Convection Oven Cookbook

1200 Days Simple and Tasty Recipes from Breakfast to Dessert for Any Appliance Model to Dazzle Your Family and Guests

Author

Johnny S. Clay

Table of Content

Introduction

Hello, and thank you for purchasing the Convection Oven Cookbook, the most comprehensive resource available for using this revolutionary kitchen appliance. This cookbook contains recipes and advice to help you make the most of your convection oven, whether you're an experienced chef or just starting in the kitchen.

The main difference between a convection oven and a regular oven may not be immediately obvious if you're unfamiliar with both appliances. Faster cooking times and even heat distribution result from convection ovens' use of a fan to circulate hot air around the food. This will result in faster and more even cooking and delicious, perfectly cooked food every time.

From savory roasts and casseroles to sweet cakes and cookies, this cookbook covers you for any occasion. There are recipes here for novices and experts, so everyone can find something they want to try.

We have included recipes and advice on how to get the most out of your convection oven. How to position your dishes for optimal cooking, how long to cook them, and other tips will be provided.

Let's dive in right now! Make delicious, evenly cooked food in a fraction of the time with the help of the Convection Oven Cookbook.

Understanding Convection Oven

A convection oven is an oven in which a fan blows hot air around the interior. Due to the uniform heat distribution, food can be cooked quickly and with less waste than in a conventional oven.

The convection oven's fan helps maintain an even temperature throughout the oven by circulating hot air around the food. This ensures no cold or hot spots in the cooking process. Cooking times and temperatures in a microwave oven are typically shorter and more manageable than in a conventional oven.

Convection ovens can either be "true" or "fan-assisted," the latter of which is more commonly found in European homes. True convection ovens have the heating element close to the fan, producing hot air right where needed. The fan in a convection oven helps the hot air get everywhere in the oven, as the heating element is placed at the bottom.

Convection ovens are ideal for baking and roasting because they allow for uniform browning of crusts and the retention of moisture in meats. They are versatile enough for steaming, broiling, and even dehydrating, among many other cooking methods.

A convection oven is helpful because it cooks food more rapidly and uniformly than a conventional oven. A convection oven is an invaluable tool for any cook, whether a professional or just trying to perfect your home cooking.

Convection Oven Accessories

Several add-ons can be used with a convection oven to expand its functionalities and elevate the quality of cooked food. Common add-ons for a convection oven include:

- ❖ **Baking stones or pizza stones:** These, crafted from non-reactive materials like ceramic or stone, are ideal for baking pizza and bread to perfection with a uniformly crisp crust.
- ❖ **Roasting racks:** These are great for using in the oven to get a nice, even browning and cooking on all sides of your meat, poultry, or vegetables.
- ❖ **Oven thermometers:** Some convection ovens have temperature variations that can affect cooking results, so these can be used to make sure the oven is at the right temperature.
- ❖ **Silicone baking mats:** The food won't stick to these mats, and you can use them over and over again on baking sheets.
- ❖ **Oven-safe meat thermometers:** These can be inserted into meat to monitor internal temperature and ensure that it is cooked to the desired level of doneness.
- ❖ **Aluminum foil:** This can be used to cover dishes during cooking to prevent over-browning or drying out.
- ❖ **Wire cooling racks:** You can use these on top of baking sheets and roasting pans to keep food from getting soggy from a lack of airflow.

Using a convection oven with the right accessories can greatly enhance your cooking outcomes.

Master Your Convection Oven

Although it may take some time to perfect your use of a convection oven, you can achieve consistent, delicious results by following a few simple guidelines. Think about these suggestions for optimizing your convection oven's use:

1. Learn to tell the difference between a convection oven and a regular oven: Using a fan to circulate hot air, convection ovens can cook food more quickly and uniformly than standard ovens. As a result, using a convection oven requires modifying traditional cooking methods, such as the timing and temperature at which you put your food in the oven.

2. It is essential to preheat your oven before using either a convection or conventional oven. Getting the oven to the right temperature before you put food in it guarantees a uniform and efficient cooking process.

3. Use equipment designed for convection ovens, such as shallow roasting pans and baking sheets with short sides. This ensures that all the food gets cooked at the same rate by allowing hot air to circulate freely around it.

4. Because convection ovens can cook food up to 25% faster than regular ovens, you must adjust your cooking times accordingly. To avoid overcooking the food, reduce the cooking time by a quarter.

5. When using a convection oven, you should reduce the temperature by about 25 degrees Fahrenheit because the appliance cooks food more quickly and evenly than a conventional oven.
6. To ensure even cooking, avoid packing the oven to capacity. When too many people are in the kitchen, the food may not cook evenly and will take longer to complete.
7. Position the oven rack in the center for optimal results in cooking uniformity. Moving food to the top rack of the oven will speed up the cooking process and produce a crispier result.

Follow these guidelines, and you can use your convection oven like a pro and cook delicious, evenly-cooked meals every time.

1.   Super Easy Egg Casserole

Prep Time: 15 minutes

Cook Time: 20 minutes

Total Time: 35 minutes

Servings: 4

Ingredients

- ➢ Six eggs whisked
- ➢ 1 cup of shredded Cheddar cheese
- ➢ Six slices bacon, diced
- ➢ Two slices of bread, cubed
- ➢ ⅓ red bell pepper, diced
- ➢ Two green onions, diced
- ➢ 3 tbsp. milk
- ➢ ½ tsp. minced garlic, or to taste
- ➢ salt and ground black pepper to taste

Directions

1. Prepare a 350°F oven (175 degrees C). Prepare a 9-by-13-inch greased baking dish.
2. After preheating the oven, combine the eggs, cheese, bacon, bread, red bell pepper, green onion, milk, garlic, salt, and black pepper until everything is well-mixed.
3. Put in the oven and bake for 20–25 minutes or until the eggs are set.

2.   Sheet Pan Breakfast Bake

Prep Time: 10 minutes

Bake Time: 37 minutes

Total Time: 47 minutes

Servings: 8

Ingredients

➢ 1 cup of Greek yogurt
➢ One ¼ cup of self-rising flour, plus more for kneading
➢ 1 tsp. carne asada seasoning
➢ cooking spray
➢ Five large eggs
➢ 1 cup of shredded Colby cheese
➢ 1 cup of frozen shredded hash brown potatoes, thawed
➢ 2 tbsp. salsa
➢ Four slices bacon
➢ green onions for garnish

Directions

1. Oven: 350 degrees Fahrenheit (175 degrees C). Apply nonstick cooking spray to a sheet pan.
2. Combine the flour, carne asada seasoning, and Greek yogurt in a medium bowl. Stir until a shaggy dough forms. Move the mixture to a surface dusted with self-rising flour, and knead for about 5 minutes or until smooth. If the dough is too sticky, keep adding flour as necessary.

3. To make a smooth dough, knead it for about five minutes.
4. To fit a sheet pan, shape the dough.
5. The dough needs 12 minutes in the preheated oven.
6. Eggs, cheese, hash browns, and salsa should be combined in a bowl while you wait.
7. Over medium-high heat, add the bacon to a large skillet and cook, occasionally stirring, for about 7 minutes, until evenly browned. To a drip line tray, remove the bacon. Let the bacon cool before roughly chopping it.
8. Sprinkle dough with egg mixture. On top, add some bacon.
9. Cook for approximately 25 minutes or until eggs are set.
10. Sliced green onions should be added after oven removal. Before serving, let the food slightly cool.

3. Slow Cooker Breakfast Burritos

Prep Time: 20 minutes

Cook Time: 3 hours 20 minutes

Total Time: 3 hours 40 minutes

Servings: 12

Ingredients

➢ 2 lbs bulk breakfast sausage
➢ One medium onion, finely diced
➢ One medium bell pepper, finely diced
➢ cooking spray
➢ 1 (16 Oz.) package of frozen shredded hash browns

- ➢ 2 ½ cups of shredded Cheddar cheese
- ➢ 12 large eggs
- ➢ 1 cup of milk
- ➢ 1 tsp. kosher salt
- ➢ ½ tsp. ground black pepper
- ➢ 12 (10-inch) flour tortillas, warmed

Directions

1. Over medium-high heat, preheat a sizable skillet. Add the sausage and cook for about 8 minutes, crumbling it up with the back of a spoon as it cooks. Add the onion and bell pepper, and cook for 5 minutes until the onion softens. Using a paper towel, dab any extra oil out of the pan. Cook the sausage for 5 to 7 minutes or until completely done. Take it off the heat. This step can be completed a day in advance.
2. Apply cooking spray to a slow cooker. Add Cheddar cheese, hash browns, and sausage mixture.
3. Thoroughly combine the eggs, milk, salt, and pepper in a bowl. Stir until everything is combined before pouring it into the slow cooker. Stirring after the first hour, cook for 6 to 8 hours on low or 3 to 4 hours on high.
4. With desired toppings, serve the mixture inside warmed tortillas.

4. Air Fryer Scrambled Eggs On The Go

Prep Time: 4 minutes

Cook Time: 6 minutes

Total Time: 10 minutes

Servings: 1

Ingredients

- cooking spray
- Two large eggs, beaten
- salt and freshly ground black pepper to taste

Directions

1. Spray nonstick cooking spray sparingly in a ramekin dish. Add the beaten eggs.
2. After adjusting the temperature to 370 degrees F (185 degrees C), the ramekin should be put into the air fryer basket.
3. Three minutes of air frying. For an additional three minutes, stir the egg mixture with a fork, fluff, and season with salt and pepper to taste. Seize the opportunity to leave.

5. Crispy Fried Poached Eggs

Prep Time: 20 minutes

Cook Time: 7 minutes

Total Time: 27 minutes

Servings: 4

Ingredients

- ➤ Four large fresh eggs
- ➤ 2 tbsp. white vinegar
- ➤ 4 cups of vegetable oil
- ➤ 1 ½ cups of all-purpose flour
- ➤ Two large eggs, lightly beaten
- ➤ 2 tsp. salt
- ➤ 1 tsp. freshly ground black pepper
- ➤ 1 ½ cups of panko bread crumbs
- ➤ 2 tbsp. diced pickled red onions
- ➤ 2 tbsp. diced green onions
- ➤ 1 tbsp. red pepper flakes for garnish or to taste

Directions

1. Over medium heat, add a saucepan's worth of cold water. Add vinegar and heat gently until simmering. For easier transfer, crack an egg into a ramekin or measuring cup while working with one egg at a time.
2. To produce a whirlpool effect, stir the water ferociously. Drop the egg into the center of the water as the whirlpool is spinning. Up until the egg white becomes opaque, gently stir while cooking. The egg should be carefully removed from the water with a slotted spoon and transferred to a plate covered with paper towels to drain.
3. Heat oil to 375 degrees F in a medium saucepan (190 degrees C).

4. Set up a dredging station in the interim with three separate bowls. Flour should be added to the first bowl. In a separate bowl, whisk two eggs with salt and pepper. The third bowl should contain breadcrumbs. Thoroughly coat the cooled egg at each station as you dip it into the flour, egg mixture, and breadcrumbs.
5. With the help of a slotted spoon, carefully place the egg into the hot oil and fry for 2 to 3 minutes or until golden brown, being careful not to overcook. On a plate covered with paper towels, drain.
6. Red pepper flakes, green onions, and pickled red onions should be used as a garnish. Serve instantly.

6.   Scrambled Egg Muffin Cup

Prep Time: 15 minutes

Cook Time: 30 minutes

Total Time: 45 minutes

Servings: 12

Ingredients
- ½ lb bulk pork sausage
- 12 eggs
- ½ cup of diced onion
- ½ cups of diced green bell pepper, or to taste
- ½ tsp. salt
- ¼ tsp. ground black pepper

- ➤ ¼ tsp. garlic powder
- ➤ ½ cup of shredded Cheddar cheese

Directions

1. Oven: 350 degrees Fahrenheit (175 degrees C). Twelve muffin tins should either be lined with paper liners or lightly greased.
2. Over medium-high heat, preheat a sizable skillet. Sausage is added and cooked for 10 to 15 minutes until it is no longer pink and crumbly. Eliminate the grease.
3. In a big bowl, whisk the eggs. Add green pepper, onion, salt, and garlic powder. Sausage and Cheddar cheese are combined. Spoon the mixture into the prepared muffin tins.
4. Bake for 20 to 25 minutes in the preheated oven or until a knife inserted close to the center comes out clean.

7.   Chocolate Cereal Breakfast Bars

Servings: 8

Ingredients

- ➤ 1 ½ cups of rolled oats
- ➤ 1 cup of puffed brown rice cereal
- ➤ ½ cup of diced raw almonds
- ➤ ⅓ cups of shredded coconut
- ➤ 3 tbsp. unsweetened cocoa powder
- ➤ 1 tsp. kosher salt
- ➤ tiny pinch of cayenne pepper
- ➤ ⅓ cups of packed brown sugar

- ➤ ½ cup of maple syrup
- ➤ 2 tbsp. vegetable oil
- ➤ 1 tbsp. water

Directions

1. Oven: 350 degrees Fahrenheit (175 degrees C). Butter should be used to grease, and parchment paper to line an 8x8 pan.
2. Rolling oats, brown rice cereal that has been puffed, almonds, coconut, cocoa powder, salt, and cayenne pepper should all be combined in a bowl.
3. Combine the brown sugar, maple syrup, vegetable oil, and water in a small pan over medium-high heat. Bring to a simmer. While stirring, allow the mixture to come to a boil.
4. Add the sugar mixture to the bowl of dry ingredients, then thoroughly combine. Please transfer to the prepared pan and lightly press the top using a spatula to smooth it out.
5. For 25 minutes, bake in the preheated oven. While the pan is still hot, make eight divisions with a spatula. Before opening the bars, allow them to reach room temperature. Additionally, you cannot wait for the knife to cool before scoring.

8.   Orange Cinnamon Rolls

Prep Time: 45 minutes

Stand Time: 10 minutes

Rise Time: 1 hour 30 minutes

Bake Time: 25 minutes

Total Time: 2 hours 50 minutes

Servings: 12

Ingredients

- ¾ cups of warm whole milk
- 1 (.25 Oz.) package of active dry yeast
- One large egg at room temperature
- One large egg yolk at room temperature
- ½ cup of unsalted butter softened
- 2 tbsp. honey
- 1 ½ tsp. freshly grated orange zest
- ¼ cups of freshly squeezed orange juice
- 3 ½ cups of all-purpose flour, divided or more as needed
- 1 ½ tsp. kosher salt
- cooking spray

Filling:

- ½ cup of unsalted butter softened
- ½ cup of light brown sugar
- 2 tsp. ground cinnamon
- 1 ½ tsp. Freshly grated orange zest

Frosting:

- 4 Oz. cream cheese, softened
- 1 cup of powdered sugar
- 1 tbsp. freshly grated orange zest
- 1 tbsp. Freshly squeezed orange juice
- ¼ tsp. kosher salt

Directions

1. Warm the milk and pour it into a stand mixer bowl with a paddle attachment for making dough. Over the milk's surface, evenly distribute the yeast. For five to ten minutes, let stand until foamy.

2. Add butter, honey, orange juice, zest, egg, and egg yolk to the yeast mixture. For about 45 seconds, beat on low to combine. Beat on low speed while adding 2 cups of flour until a wet dough forms, about 1 minute. Shut off the mixer and select the dough hook attachment. Beat on medium for 7 to 10 minutes, adding 1 1/2 cups of flour and salt until the dough is soft and elastic. Use as little flour as possible to create a soft dough when adding 1/2 cup if necessary. The dough must be extremely sticky.

3. Place a ball from the dough in a big, greased bowl. Wrapped in plastic, leave covered at room temperature for about an hour or until it has doubled in size.

4. Combine the butter, brown sugar, cinnamon, and orange zest in a bowl for the filling. Mix with a spatula for about a minute or until smooth and creamy. Set apart.

5. The dough is laid down, then transferred to a floured surface. A large 10 x 18-inch rectangle of dough should be rolled out. Filling over the dough's surface leaves a 1/2-inch border along the long top edge.

6. Roll the dough in a log shape away from you, pinching the seam shut.

7. The dough log should be cut into 12 equal rolls 1 1/2 inches wide. Rolls should be placed in a greased 13 x 9-inch baking dish. Cover loosely with plastic wrap and leave to rise for 30

to 45 minutes at room temperature or until puffy and nearly doubled in size.
8. Set the oven to 375°F for preheating (190 degrees C).
9. Rolls should bake for 22 to 25 minutes in a preheated oven until golden brown.
10.   The frosting should be made while the rolls are baking. Combine cream cheese, powdered sugar, orange zest, and salt in the bowl of a stand mixer with the paddle attachment. Beat for two to three minutes at medium-high speed or until smooth and creamy.
11.   Take rolls out of the oven and place them on a wire rack. Spread frosting evenly over the rolls after cooling them for two minutes. Serve hot.

9.   Minute Breakfast Burrito

Prep Time: 5 minutes

Total Time: 5 minutes

Servings: 1

Ingredients
➢ Two eggs
➢ 2 tbsp. salsa
➢ One slice of reduced-fat American cheese
➢ One tortilla

Directions

1. Spray nonstick cooking spray inside a cereal bowl. In the bowl, crack the eggs, add the salsa, and stir. Cook on high for 1 minute, stir, then continue cooking for one more minute or until the mixture thickens.
2. The egg mixture should be placed on the cheese in the tortilla's center. Head for the car after wrapping everything up like a burrito.

10. Southwestern Breakfast Burrito

Prep Time: 5 minutes

Cook Time: 5 minutes

Total Time: 10 minutes

Servings: 2

Ingredients

➢ Two low carb whole wheat tortillas
➢ Four eggs
➢ 2 tbsp. cream
➢ 1 pinch salt and white pepper
➢ ¼ tsp. cumin powder
➢ ½ tbsp. butter
➢ 1 ½ tbsp. salsa, chunky style
➢ 2 Oz. Cheddar cheese, shredded

Directions

1. Beat the eggs in a mixing bowl with the cream, salsa, cumin, and a dash of salt and pepper.
2. Melt the butter in a nonstick skillet over medium-high heat before scrambling the eggs. Add the cheese and fold it in until it melts just before they are set.
3. On a level surface, spread out the tortillas. Place the eggs on the bottom third of each tortilla, dividing them equally between the two. The bottom third is folded over and tucked in. Before rolling up, fold the two sides in. Serve.

11. Air Fryer Hash Brown "Toast"

Prep Time: 5 minutes

Cook Time: 15 minutes

Total Time: 20 minutes

Servings: 4

Ingredients

➢ 4 frozen hash brown patties

Topping

➢ Two avocados
➢ salt and freshly cracked ground black pepper to taste
➢ 2 tsp. freshly squeezed lemon juice, or to taste
➢ 1 tbsp. butter
➢ Four large eggs

- ➢ 1 cup of arugula, or to taste
- ➢ 2 tsp. spicy honey, or to taste

Directions

1. The air fryer to 400 degrees C. (200 degrees C).
2. In the air fryer basket, arrange four frozen hash brown potato patties in a single layer.
3. Cook in the hot air fryer for 13 to 15 minutes, turning once halfway through, until golden and crispy.
4. In a big skillet over medium heat, melt 1 tbsp. Of butter. In the skillet, crack eggs and cook for about a minute or until the edges are opaque. Cook under cover for about 4 minutes on low heat or until the whites are completely set.
5. Salt, pepper, and lemon juice are added to mashed avocados in a bowl. Hot hash browns should be covered with mashed avocado. Fry an egg and add some arugula to the top of each. Add a hot honey drizzle and freshly cracked black pepper to taste.

12. Breakfast Pork Cutlets

Prep Time: 20 minutes

Cook Time: 5 minutes

Total Time: 25 minutes

Servings: 2 servings

Ingredients
Spice Mix:

- 1/4 tsp. whole fennel seeds
- 1/2 tsp. freshly ground black pepper
- 1/2 tsp. dried poultry seasoning
- 1/4 tsp. freshly ground nutmeg
- 1/4 tsp. garlic powder
- One pinch of cayenne pepper

Cutlet:

- 2 (6-8-Oz.) boneless center-cut pork chops, trimmed
- 1 1/2 tsp. kosher salt
- 2 tsp. maple syrup
- 1/2 cup of fine dry breadcrumbs
- 2 tbsp. olive oil
- 1 tbsp. butter

Directions

1. Fennel seeds should be crushed and then transferred to a small bowl. Black pepper, nutmeg, garlic powder, cayenne, and poultry seasoning are stirred.
2. Make several shallow vertical cuts through the fat on the edges of each pork chop. Utilizing meat labor or another heavy flat object, place each chop between 2 pieces of plastic wrap and lb to 1/4-inch thickness. Toss onto a plate.
3. Chops are seasoned on both sides with salt and a spice mixture. Apply about half a tsp of maple syrup to each side of the chops.
4. Sprinkle breadcrumbs on one side of each chop and press firmly. Repeat on the other side.
5. In a nonstick skillet over medium-high heat, melt butter and olive oil. Pork cutlets should be browned and crisp on both

sides after cooking for about 2 minutes per side, turning once the meat is no longer pink in the center. A near-center-inserted instant-read thermometer should register 145 degrees Fahrenheit (63 degrees C).

13. French Toast

Prep Time: 5 minutes

Cook Time: 10 minutes

Total Time: 15 minutes

Servings: 3

Ingredients

- ⅔ cups of milk
- Two large eggs
- 1 tsp. vanilla extract
- ¼ tsp. ground cinnamon
- salt to taste
- Six thick slices of bread
- 1 tbsp. unsalted butter, or more as needed

Directions

1. Amass all the ingredients.
2. Combine the salt, vanilla, cinnamon, milk, and eggs in a small bowl.
3. Heat a griddle or skillet over medium-high heat with a little butter.
4. Immerse the bread on both sides in the egg mixture.

5. Cook for three to four minutes on each side in the hot skillet until golden. Hot food.

14. Easy Sausage Gravy and Biscuits

Prep Time: 5 minutes

Cook Time: 10 minutes

Total Time: 15 minutes

Servings: 8

Ingredients

> ➤ 1 (16 Oz.) can of refrigerated jumbo buttermilk biscuits
> ➤ 1 (9.6 Oz.) package of Jimmy Dean® Original Hearty Pork Sausage Crumbles
> ➤ ¼ cups of flour
> ➤ 2 ½ cups of milk
> ➤ salt and freshly ground black pepper to taste

Directions

1. Oven: 350 degrees Fahrenheit (175 degrees C). Space the biscuits 1 to 2 inches apart on an ungreased cookie sheet. Bake in the preheated oven for 13 to 15 minutes or until the top is golden brown.
2. In the meantime, heat sausage thoroughly in a sizable skillet over medium-high heat for 5 to 6 minutes, stirring frequently.
3. Flour should be thoroughly mixed in. Till the gravy thickens and boils, gradually add milk while stirring constantly.

Simmer and stir for two more minutes with the heat reduced to medium-low. Salt and pepper should be used to taste.

4. Bread is cut in half. Eight plates should each have two halves. Add about 1/3 cup of gravy on top.

15. Quick and Easy Home Fries

Prep Time: 5 minutes

Cook Time: 20 minutes

Total Time: 25 minutes

Servings: 4

Ingredients

➢ Three medium russet potatoes, cubed
➢ 3 tbsp. butter or margarine
➢ salt and ground black pepper to taste

Directions

1. Potato cubes should be thoroughly drained after a cold water rinse.
2. Over medium heat, melt butter in a sizable skillet. Season the potatoes in the skillet with salt and pepper, then stir to combine. For 10 minutes, cook with a cover.
3. After about 10 minutes, remove the lid and continue to cook while frequently turning the food until it is crisp and brown on all sides.

16. Best Monkey Bread

Prep Time: 15 minutes

Cook Time: 40 minutes

Additional Time: 10 minutes

Total Time: 1 hour 5 minutes

Servings: 15

Ingredients

- 1 cup of white sugar
- 2 tsp. ground cinnamon
- 3 (12 Oz.) packages of refrigerated biscuit dough
- ½ cup of diced walnuts
- ½ cup of raisins
- ½ cup of margarine
- 1 cup of packed brown sugar

Directions

1. Amass all the ingredients.
2. Three hundred fifty degrees Fahrenheit should be set for the oven (175 degrees C). Grease a Bundt® pan or one 9- or 10-inch tube pan.
3. In a plastic bag, combine white sugar and cinnamon. Create biscuit quarters. In the sugar-cinnamon mixture, stir 6 to 8 biscuit pieces.
4. In the bottom of the prepared pan, arrange the pieces. Continue doing this until the biscuits are coated and in the

pan. If using, distribute the walnuts and raisins throughout the biscuit pieces.

5. In a small saucepan, melt margarine and the brown sugar over medium heat—1 minute of boiling. Give the biscuits a drizzle.

6. Thirty-five minutes of baking in a preheated oven. Bread should be turned onto a plate after cooling the pan for 10 minutes. Stop cutting! Just pulling separates the bread.

17. Basic Biscuits

Prep Time: 15 minutes

Cook Time: 10 minutes

Total Time: 25 minutes

Servings: 10

Ingredients

- ➢ 2 cups of all-purpose flour
- ➢ 1 tbsp. baking powder
- ➢ ½ tsp. salt
- ➢ ½ cup of shortening
- ➢ ¾ cups of cold milk

Directions

1. Then, assemble the ingredients and heat the oven to 450 degrees F. (230 degrees C).

2. Sift flour, baking powder, and salt together in a sizable mixing bowl. Stir in the shortening with a fork or pastry blender until the mixture resembles coarse crumbs.
3. While whisking with a fork, pour milk into the flour mixture. Milk should be added until the dough is soft, moist, and removed from the bowl's edge.
4. Turn the dough onto a lightly dusted surface and quickly knead it 5 to 7 times.
5. Cut biscuit shapes from a 1/2-inch thick rolled-out dough with a floured cookie cutter. Repeat the rolling and cutting steps, then press any leftover dough together.
6. Bake biscuits for 10 minutes, or until golden brown, on ungreased baking sheets in a preheated oven.

18. Fluffy French Toast

Prep Time: 10 minutes

Cook Time: 20 minutes

Total Time: 30 minutes

Servings: 12

Ingredients

➢ ¼ cups of all-purpose flour
➢ 1 cup of milk
➢ Three eggs
➢ 1 tbsp. white sugar
➢ 1 tsp. vanilla extract

- ½ tsp. ground cinnamon
- 1 pinch salt
- 12 thick slices of bread

Directions

1. Count the flour into a sizable mixing bowl. Blend milk in gradually. Stir in the eggs, sugar, vanilla, cinnamon, and salt until smooth.
2. Over medium heat, warm a griddle or frying pan that has been lightly oiled.
3. Bread slices in milk mixture until completely submerged.
4. Cook the bread on the heated grill or pan in batches until golden brown on both sides—hot food.

19.   Easy French Toast Casserole

Prep Time: 15 minutes

Cook Time: 30 minutes

Additional Time: 8 hours

Total Time: 8 hours 45 minutes

Servings: 8

Ingredients
French Toast:

- 1 cup of brown sugar
- ½ cup of unsalted butter

- 1 (8 Oz.), a loaf of crusty French bread, cut into bite-sized pieces or more as needed
- 2 cups of milk
- Six large eggs
- 2 tsp. vanilla extract

Topping:

- 1 tbsp. Brown sugar, or to taste
- ¼ tsp. the ground cinnamon, or to taste

Directions

1. Clean and grease a 9x13-inch baking pan.
2. French toast preparation: Over medium-low heat, combine brown sugar and butter and constantly stir for 2 to 4 minutes, until the butter has melted and the sugar has completely dissolved.
3. Fill the baking dish with the butter-brown sugar mixture. Add a layer of 1 1/2 to 2 inches of French bread slices on top.
4. In a bowl, thoroughly combine the milk, eggs, and vanilla. Pour over the bread pieces, then press with a spatula to help the bread soak up the liquid. Refrigerate the dish for eight hours the next day by wrapping it in plastic.
5. Remove the French toast from the fridge and discard the plastic wrap before baking. Set the oven to 450°F for preheating (230 degrees C).
6. Prepare to top: In a small bowl, combine brown sugar and cinnamon. Add some on top of the French toast.

7. About 30 minutes into baking the casserole in the oven, check if the top is browning too much, and cover it with aluminum foil.
8. To serve, slice into squares and flip onto plates.

20. Gingerbread Cinnamon Rolls

Prep Time: 45 minutes

Rise Time: 2 hours 25 minutes

Bake Time: 25 minutes

Cool Time: 15 minutes

Total Time: 3 hours 50 minutes

Servings: 12

Ingredients
Dough:

➢ ½ cup of warm whole milk (110 degrees F (43 degrees C))
➢ 3 tbsp. molasses
➢ 1 (.25 Oz.) envelope of active dry yeast
➢ ¼ cups of granulated sugar
➢ 2 tsp. kosher salt
➢ Four ¾ cups of all-purpose flour, divided or more as needed
➢ ½ cup of sour cream
➢ 6 tbsp. unsalted butter softened
➢ One large egg, lightly beaten
➢ cooking spray

Filling:

- ½ cup of unsalted butter at room temperature
- 1 cup of firmly packed light brown sugar
- 1 tbsp. molasses
- 2 tsp. ground cinnamon
- 2 tsp. ground ginger
- ½ tsp. ground cloves

Glaze:

- 4 Oz. cream cheese at room temperature
- 4 tbsp. unsalted butter at room temperature
- 1 ½ cups of powdered sugar
- ½ tsp. vanilla extract
- 1 tbsp. whole milk, or more as needed

Directions

1. In a small bowl, stir together the yeast, molasses, and warm milk until well combined. For about five minutes, let sit until foamy.
2. Add the sugar, salt, and 4 1/2 cups of flour to the work bowl of a stand mixer with the paddle attachment. Beat at low speed for approximately 15 seconds to combine.
3. Add butter, egg, sour cream, and milk mixture while the mixer is at low speed. Beat steadily for one to two minutes or until dough forms.
4. Adapt a dough hook as your new attachment. Beat for 6 to 9 minutes on medium-low speed or until dough is smooth and elastic; if necessary, add 1/4 cup of flour by the tsp. Ful.

5. Turn the dough to coat it in a sizable bowl greased with cooking spray. Wrap in a fresh kitchen towel. Allow dough to rise for one to two hours in a warm, draft-free environment.

6. Using cooking spray, coat a 13 x 9-inch pan. Punch down the dough just a little. Roll out the dough to a rectangle measuring 18 x 10 inches on a lightly dusted surface.

7. Cover the dough for the filling with 1/2 cup of butter. Combine the brown sugar, molasses, cinnamon, ginger, and cloves well in a small bowl. Over butter, sprinkle evenly.

8. Roll the dough into a log beginning with the long side; pinch the seam to seal.

9. Twelve rolls should be made. In the prepared pan, arrange the rolls. For 45 to 60 minutes, cover and allow the dough to rise in a warm, draft-free area until it has doubled in size.

10. Oven: 350 degrees Fahrenheit (175 degrees C).

11. Bake uncovered in the oven for 25 to 30 minutes or until golden brown. Allow the pan to cool on a wire rack for 15 minutes.

12. Add cream cheese and 4 tbsp. Butter to the paddle attachment-equipped stand mixer bowl and beat on medium speed for 1 to 2 minutes or until smooth. Milk, vanilla, and powdered sugar should be added. For about a minute, blend at medium speed. Add milk to 1 tsp at a time to achieve the desired consistency if necessary.

13. Over warm rolls, spread the glaze.

21. Loaded Reuben Totchos

Prep Time: 15 minutes

Cook Time: 35 minutes

Total Time: 50 minutes

Servings: 12

Ingredients

- ➢ 1 (32 Oz.) package of frozen fried potato nuggets
- ➢ 6 Oz. corned beef, diced (1 cup)
- ➢ ½ cup of sauerkraut, drained
- ➢ 1 cup of shredded Swiss cheese (4 oz.)
- ➢ 1 cup of shredded Colby and Monterey Jack cheese (4 oz.)
- ➢ ½ cup of Thousand Island salad dressing
- ➢ 1 tbsp. spicy brown mustard
- ➢ 2 tbsp. diced green onion
- ➢ ¼ tsp. caraway seeds, toasted

Directions

1. Set the oven to 450°F for preheating (230 degrees C). Use foil to cover a baking sheet.
2. On the prepared baking sheet, spread the potato nuggets for 28 to 32 minutes in the oven or until golden brown.
3. Corned beef, sauerkraut, Swiss cheese, Colby, and Monterey Jack cheese are some delicious toppings for potato nuggets. After 5-8 minutes in the oven, the cheese should be melted.

4. Sprinkle with mustard and Thousand Island dressing. Add some caraway seeds and green onions.

22. Air-Fried Raspberry Brie Bites

Prep Time: 20 minutes

Cook Time: 15 minutes

Total Time: 35 minutes

Servings: 16

Ingredients

- ➢ 1 (8 Oz.) round Brie cheese
- ➢ 1 (8 Oz.), the package of phyllo dough, thawed
- ➢ 1 cup of raspberry jam
- ➢ 1 cup of butter, melted
- ➢ 2 tbsp. honey
- ➢ flakey salt to taste

Directions

1. Cut the brie into squares between 1 and 1 1/2 inches wide and 1/2 inches thick.
2. One sheet of phyllo dough should be vertically rolled out on a sizable work surface. After brushing the dough's bottom half with melted butter, fold the top half over the bottom.
3. Place one piece of cheese in the bottom center of the dough, about 2 inches from the edges. On the cheese, spread about two tsp of raspberry jam. The remaining dough should be covered in melted butter.

4. Over the cheese, fold the bottom 2 inches of the dough inward, followed by the sides. The remaining dough should be brushed with more butter. Carefully roll the filling upward until it is completely encased. Put the top in the air fryer and add more butter.
5. Achieve 375°F in the air fryer (190 degrees C).
6. Air fry in batches until golden brown, 4 to 5 minutes, to prevent crowding. Add some flaky salt and a thin honey drizzle as garnish. Serve instantly.

23.   Feta-Spinach Puff Pastry Bites

Prep Time: 15 minutes

Cook Time: 15 minutes

Cool Time: 5 minutes

Total Time: 35 minutes

Servings: 24

Ingredients

- ➢ nonstick cooking spray
- ➢ One sheet of frozen puff pastry, thawed in the refrigerator
- ➢ ¾ cups of mayonnaise
- ➢ 1 (6 Oz.) container of crumbled feta cheese
- ➢ ½ cup of freshly grated Parmesan cheese
- ➢ One (10 Oz.) package of frozen diced spinach, thawed and drained
- ➢ Two cloves garlic, minced

➢ ¼ tsp. ground black pepper

Directions

1. Set the oven to 375°F for preheating (180 degrees C). A 24-cup mini muffin pan (or two 12-cup mini muffin pans) should be sprayed with nonstick cooking spray before use.
2. Using a rolling pin and a lightly dusted surface, create a rectangle from the frozen but still cold puff pastry sheet. Use a pizza cutter to cut into 24 (roughly 2 1/2 inch) squares. Prick each mini muffin pan cup with a fork after gently pressing a square of puff pastry into it.
3. Spinach, garlic, pepper, feta cheese, Parmesan cheese, and mayonnaise should all be combined in a bowl.
4. Be careful not to overfill the cups as you evenly distribute the feta-spinach mixture.
5. Bake for 15 to 16 minutes, until the pastry is golden brown and puffy in the corners, in the preheated oven.
6. Before transferring the bites to a serving dish, let them cool in the pan on a wire rack for five minutes.

24. Baked Ham and Cheese Sliders

Prep Time: 15 minutes

Cook Time: 20 minutes

Total Time: 35 minutes

Servings: 24

Ingredients

- ¾ cups of melted butter
- 1 ½ tbsp. Dijon mustard
- 1 ½ tsp. Worcestershire sauce
- 1 ½ tbsp. poppy seeds
- 1 tbsp. dried minced onion
- 24 mini sandwich rolls
- 1 lb thinly sliced cooked deli ham
- 1 lb thinly sliced Swiss cheese

Directions

1. Amass all the ingredients.
2. Oven: 350 degrees Fahrenheit (175 degrees C). Clean and grease a 9x13-inch baking pan.
3. Combine the butter, Dijon mustard, Worcestershire sauce, poppy seeds, and dried onion in a bowl.
4. Separate the tops from the bottoms of the rolls, then layer the bottom pieces in the baking dish that has been prepared. The rolls should be covered with about half the ham, followed by a layer of Swiss cheese and the remaining ham slices.
5. Sandwiches should have roll tops on them. Spread the rolls with the mustard mixture evenly.
6. Bake in the oven for about 20 minutes or until the rolls brown lightly and the cheese has melted. Slice through the ham and cheese layers into individual rolls to serve.

25. Fried Mozzarella Cheese Sticks

Prep Time: 15 minutes

Cook Time: 10 minutes

Total Time: 25 minutes

Servings: 8

Ingredients

- Two large eggs, beaten
- ¼ cups of water
- 1 ½ cups of Italian seasoned bread crumbs
- ½ tsp. garlic salt
- ⅔ cups of all-purpose flour
- ⅓ cups of cornstarch
- 2 cups of oil for frying or as needed
- 1 (16 Oz.) package of mozzarella cheese sticks

Directions

1. Amass all the ingredients.
2. In a small bowl, combine water and eggs. In a medium bowl, combine the bread crumbs and the garlic salt. In a third bowl, combine the cornstarch and flour.
3. Oil in a large, heavy saucepan is heated to 365 degrees F (185 degrees C).
4. Shake off excess flour after dredging a mozzarella stick in it. Dip in the egg mixture. The excess egg should drip back into the bowl as you lift. Coat with bread crumbs and press. On a plate or wire rack, place the breaded mozzarella stick. Repeat with the rest of the mozzarella sticks.

5. Use a spider spoon or a pair of tongs to place three to four mozzarella sticks into the hot oil. About 30 seconds of frying time until golden brown. Drain on paper towels after removing from heat. Continually fry the remaining mozzarella sticks.

26. Bisquick Sausage Balls

Prep Time: 15 minutes

Cook Time: 25 minutes

Total Time: 40 minutes

Servings: 16

Ingredients

➢ 6 cups of baking mix
➢ 2 lbs shredded extra-sharp Cheddar cheese
➢ 1 lb sage-flavored pork sausage at room temperature
➢ 1 lb hot pork sausage at room temperature

Directions

1. Amass all the ingredients.
2. Set the oven to 300 degrees F. (150 degrees C). Bakeware should be greased.
3. Combine the baking mix, Cheddar cheese, and hot and sage-flavored pork sausages in a bowl.
4. Shape the sausage mixture into one 1/2-inch ball and place them on the baking sheets that have been prepared.

5. Bake for 25 to 30 minutes in a preheated oven or until the outside is browned and the center is no longer pink.

27. Air Fryer Pasta Chips

Prep Time: 5 minutes

Cook Time: 40 minutes

Additional Time: 5 minutes

Total Time: 50 minutes

Servings: 8

Ingredients

> 2 cups of farfalle pasta
> 1 tbsp. olive oil
> ½ cup of grated Parmesan cheese
> 1 tsp. garlic powder
> 1 tsp. Italian seasoning
> ½ tsp. salt

Directions

1. Large pasta should be cooked for about 8 minutes, occasionally stirring, in lightly salted water that has been brought to a boil. Rinse, but do not drain. Observe for two minutes.
2. Set an air fryer to 400 degrees Fahrenheit (200 degrees C).
3. Olive oil should be drizzled over the pasta as it is being prepared, then the Parmesan cheese, garlic powder, Italian

seasoning, and salt should all be thoroughly combined. Place one layer of one-fourth of the pasta in the air fryer basket.

4. Cook in the preheated air fryer for five minutes, then flip and cook for 2 to 3 minutes. Transfer to a plate lined with paper towels, separating any clumped-together pasta chips, and allow to cool completely. With the remaining pasta, repeat.

28.   Basic Keto Cheese Crisps

Prep Time: 5 minutes

Cook Time: 10 minutes

Additional Time: 5 minutes

Total Time: 20 minutes

Servings: 4

Ingredients

➢ 1 cup of shredded Cheddar cheese

Directions

1. Oven: 400 degrees Fahrenheit (200 degrees C). Put parchment paper on two baking trays.
2. Shred copious quantities of cheese.
3. Place the cheese on the preheated baking sheets in 24 small heaps.

4. For about 7 minutes, bake in the preheated oven until golden brown. Remove from baking sheets and allow to cool for 5 to 10 minutes.

29. Mango Salsa

Prep Time: 15 minutes

Additional Time: 30 minutes

Total Time: 45 minutes

Servings: 8

Ingredients

- ➢ One mango - peeled, seeded, and diced
- ➢ ¼ cups of finely diced red bell pepper
- ➢ One green onion, diced
- ➢ One fresh jalapeno chile pepper, finely diced
- ➢ 2 tbsp. diced cilantro
- ➢ 2 tbsp. lime juice
- ➢ 1 tbsp. lemon juice

Directions

1. Ingredient gathering.
2. Combine the mango, red bell pepper, green onion, cilantro, jalapeno, and lime and lemon juices in a medium bowl.
3. Ingredients should be thoroughly combined. At least 30 minutes should pass while covered before serving.

30. Air Fryer Celery Root Fries

Prep Time: 10 minutes

Cook Time: 18 minutes

Additional Time: 20 minutes

Total Time: 48 minutes

Servings: 4

Ingredients

- ½ celeriac (celery root), peeled and cut into 1/2-inch sticks
- Three cups of water
- 1 tbsp. lime juice

Mayo Sauce:

- ⅓ cups of vegan mayonnaise
- 1 tbsp. brown mustard
- 1 tsp. powdered horseradish
- 1 tbsp. olive oil
- One pinch of salt and ground black pepper to taste

Directions

1. Fill a bowl with celery root. Lime juice and water are added. Twenty minutes should pass after mixing.
2. The air fryer should be preheated to 400 degrees F. (200 degrees C).
3. Produce the mayo sauce. Horseradish powder, vegan mayonnaise, and mustard should all be combined. Refrigerate until needed while covered.

4. The celery root sticks should be drained, dried, and put back into a bowl. Salt and pepper the fries after drizzling oil over them. Evenly coat with a toss.
5. The air fryer basket should now contain celery root. Cook for approximately 10 minutes, checking for doneness every few minutes. Fries should be crisp and browned after another 8 minutes of cooking, so shake the basket.
6. Serve vegan mayo alongside the fries right away.

31. Blue Cheese and Pear Tartlets

Prep Time: 10 minutes

Cook Time: 15 minutes

Total Time: 25 minutes

Servings: 15

Ingredients

➤ One ripe pear - peeled, cored, and diced
➤ 4 Oz. blue cheese, crumbled
➤ 2 tbsp. light cream
➤ ground black pepper to taste
➤ 1 (1.9 Oz.) package of mini phyllo tart shells

Directions

1. Oven: 350 degrees Fahrenheit (175 degrees C).
2. Pear, blue cheese, and cream should all be combined in a baking dish. Add pepper for flavor. Put the mixture inside the phyllo shells.

3. For 15 minutes, bake in a preheated oven. Provide hot.

32.   Air Fryer Ravioli

Prep Time: 10 minutes

Cook Time: 10 minutes

Total Time: 20 minutes

Servings: 3

Ingredients

- ➢ One large egg
- ➢ 1 tbsp. water
- ➢ ¼ cups of Italian-style bread crumbs
- ➢ ¼ cups of freshly grated Pecorino Romano cheese
- ➢ 1 (9 Oz.) package of refrigerated spinach and mozzarella ravioli
- ➢ olive oil cooking spray
- ➢ 1 cup of marinara sauce, heated

Directions

1. As the manufacturer directs, heat an air fryer to 350 degrees F (175 degrees C).
2. In a small bowl, combine the water and the egg. On a plate, mix the Pecorino Romano cheese and bread crumbs. One ravioli should be dipped in the beaten egg mixture, then into the bread crumbs, coating it thoroughly. Bread the remaining ravioli, then arrange them on a plate. Apply cooking spray sparingly to the ravioli.

3. Fill the air fryer basket with as many ravioli as you can without them touching.
4. Cook for 6 minutes in the preheated air fryer before flipping the ravioli and cooking for another 4 minutes. Repeat with the remaining ravioli after taking them out of the air fryer. Serve with your preferred marinara sauce on the side.

33. Air Fryer Mac and Cheese Balls

Prep Time: 15 minutes

Cook Time: 10 minutes

Additional Time: 3 hours

Total Time: 3 hours 25 minutes

Servings: 24

Ingredients

> 6 cups of water
> 1 (7.25 Oz.) package of macaroni and cheese dinner mix
> ¼ cups of milk
> 4 tbsp. margarine
> ¾ cups of shredded sharp Cheddar cheese
> nonstick cooking spray
> ½ cup of panko bread crumbs
> ½ cup of seasoned bread crumbs
> ½ tsp. salt
> ½ tsp. garlic powder
> Two eggs, beaten

Directions

1. Over high heat, pour water into a bowl and bring to a boil. Add the mac and cheese from the dinner package. Stirring occasionally; cook for 7 to 8 minutes or until tender. Rinse, not drain. Once more, add the milk, margarine, and cheese sauce to the pot. Cheddar cheese should be added and stirred until melted.

2. Put macaroni and cheese in the fridge for two to eight hours to get it firm.

3. Scoop macaroni and cheese into one 1/2-inch ball, then arrange them on a cookie sheet covered with parchment paper—one hour of freezing.

4. As the manufacturer directs, heat an air fryer to 350 degrees F (175 degrees C). They were cooking nonstick spray into the basket.

5. Combine panko, bread crumbs, garlic powder, salt, and oil in a medium bowl. Before dipping each ball in the panko mixture, beat the eggs.

6. Ensure the mac and cheese balls are not touching as you place them in the air fryer basket; if necessary, cook them in batches.

7. For 6 to 8 minutes, cook in the air fryer that has been heated. Fry on the other side for 3 to 4 minutes until golden brown.

34. Crispy Crab Rangoon

Prep Time: 25 minutes

Cook Time: 15 minutes

Total Time: 40 minutes

Servings: 10

Ingredients

- ➤ Two (8 Oz.) packages of cream cheese, softened
- ➤ 1 lb crabmeat, shredded
- ➤ 3 tbsp. dark soy sauce
- ➤ 1 tsp. minced fresh ginger root
- ➤ ½ tsp. diced fresh cilantro
- ➤ ½ tsp. dried parsley
- ➤ ½ tsp. minced garlic
- ➤ 1 (14 Oz.) package of small won ton wrappers
- ➤ 1-quart oil for frying

Directions

1. Combine the cream cheese, crabmeat, ginger, cilantro, parsley, soy sauce, and these additional ingredients in a bowl.
2. Oil should be heated to 360°F in a sizable, heavy skillet or deep fryer (180 degrees C).
3. Fill the center of a wonton wrapper with 1/2 to 1 tsp. Of the cream cheese mixture as the oil is heating. Wet the edge of the wrapper, then bring two corners together over the filling to form a triangle. Join the remaining two corners by pulling them up, and then firmly press to seal. To make additional wontons, repeat. Until the oil is hot, place the prepared wontons beneath a paper towel that is only slightly moist.

4. Fry 3 to 4 wontons at a time, in batches, in hot oil until golden and crispy, 1 to 2 minutes, flipping halfway through. Wontons should be moved to a plate lined with paper towels to drain—hot food.

35. Air Fryer Egg Rolls

Prep Time: 30 minutes

Cook Time: 15 minutes

Total Time: 45 minutes

Servings: 16

Ingredients

- 2 cups of frozen corn, thawed
- One (15 Oz.) can of black beans, drained and rinsed
- 1 (13.5 Oz.) can of spinach, drained
- 1 ½ cups of shredded jalapeno Jack cheese
- 1 cup of sharp Cheddar cheese, shredded
- One (for Oz.) can of diced green chiles, drained
- Four green onions, sliced
- 1 tsp. salt
- 1 tsp. ground cumin
- 1 tsp. chili powder
- One (16 Oz.) package of egg roll wrappers
- cooking spray

Directions

1. For the filling, combine corn, beans, spinach, jalapeno Jack cheese, Cheddar cheese, green chiles, green onions, salt, cumin, and chili powder in a sizable bowl.
2. The egg roll wrapper is laid at an angle. All four edges should be lightly dampened with water using your finger. Put a quarter cup or so of the filling in the middle of the wrapper. Tuck in the sides and fold one corner over the filling to form a roll. Apply cooking spray to each egg roll and repeat with the remaining wrappers.
3. Bring an air fryer up to 390 degrees Fahrenheit (199 degrees C). Ensure the egg rolls are not touching as you place them in the basket; cook them in batches if necessary. Cook for an additional 4 minutes after flipping after 8 minutes of cooking the first side.

36. Baked Hawaiian Sandwiches

Prep Time: 15 minutes

Cook Time: 20 minutes

Total Time: 35 minutes

Servings: 24

Ingredients

➤ 24 Hawaiian bread rolls, split
➤ 12 thin slices of honey-cured deli ham, halved
➤ 12 slices Swiss cheese, halved

- ➤ 12 thin slices deli smoked turkey, halved
- ➤ 12 thin slices of provolone cheese, halved
- ➤ ½ cup of butter
- ➤ ¼ cups of white sugar
- ➤ ¼ cups of dried onion flakes
- ➤ 2 tbsp. poppy seeds
- ➤ 1 tbsp. honey mustard

Directions

1. Set a rack in the bottom half of the oven and heat it to 400 degrees F. (200 degrees C).
2. Place the Hawaiian roll bottom halves on a baking sheet. Each roll bottom should have a half slice of smoked turkey, Swiss cheese, ham, and provolone cheese. To assemble sandwiches, place the top halves on top of each bottom.
3. Brush butter over the tops of each sandwich. Melt sugar, dried onion flakes, poppy seeds, and honey mustard in a small saucepan over low heat. Stir for about two minutes until the mixture is smooth and the sugar has dissolved.
4. Sandwiches should bake for about 15 minutes on the lower rack of a preheated oven or until the tops are golden brown and the fillings are hot.

37. Air Fryer Tostones

Prep Time: 15 minutes

Cook Time: 15 minutes

Total Time: 30 minutes

Servings: 4

Ingredients

- ➤ Two green (unripe) plantains
- ➤ olive oil cooking spray
- ➤ 3 cups of water, or as needed
- ➤ salt to taste

Directions

1. Set an air fryer to 400 degrees Fahrenheit (200 degrees C).
2. Cut the plantains' tips off. Ensure to only cut through the thick skin, not the plantain flesh. Make a vertical cut in the skin from end to end. Cut the plantain into 1-inch chunks while it is still in the peel. Starting at the slit you made, peel the skin off each chunk.
3. Put the plantain chunks in the basket of your air fryer and spray them with olive oil. 5 minutes of air frying. Get a bowl of salted water ready in the meantime.
4. Use tongs to remove the fried plantains from the air fryer. Use a stoner to smash to about a half-inch thickness (plantain smasher). Smash the rest of the tostones and soak them in a bowl of salted water.
5. Tostones are removed from the salted water and dried with paper towels.
6. Add tostones to the air fryer in batches, filling the basket with one layer each time. The tops are sprayed with olive oil spray, salt and air-fried for five minutes. Turn with tongs and apply olive oil spray to the reverse side. Add salt to the dish. For 4 to 5 minutes, air fry until golden and crisp.

38. Fried Empanadas

Prep Time: 50 minutes

Cook Time: 1 hour 10 minutes

Additional Time: 1 hour

Total Time: 3 hours

Servings: 24

Ingredients
Dough:

- 4 ½ cups of all-purpose flour
- 1 ½ tsp. salt
- ½ cup of shortening
- One ¼ cup of water, or as needed

Filling:

- 2 tbsp. olive oil
- One small onion, diced
- 1 ½ lbs ground beef
- 2 tbsp. paprika
- 1 tbsp. Cumin
- ½ tsp. ground black pepper
- 1 pinch salt
- ½ cup of raisins
- 1 tbsp. white vinegar
- Two large hard-cooked eggs, peeled and diced

For Frying:

➤ One quart oil for frying or as needed

Directions

1. Produce the dough: Combine the flour and salt in a medium bowl. Using a pastry blender, blend shortening into the mixture until it resembles coarse crumbs—a few tbsp. Of water at a time, stir in with a fork, which will bring the mixture together. Slightly flatten after patting into a ball. Refrigerate for an hour after wrapping in plastic wrap.

2. Create the filling while the dough chills: Warm oil in a big skillet over medium heat. Cook for about 5 minutes, then add onion. Cook and stir the beef, paprika, cumin, pepper, and salt for 5 to 7 minutes or until it is browned and crumbly. Remove any extra grease, then add the raisins and vinegar. For approximately 1 hour, cover and chill.

3. Refrigerated dough and filling should be removed. Make 24 2-inch balls out of the dough. Incorporate hard-boiled eggs into the filling.

4. To 365 degrees F, deep-fryer oil should be heated (180 degrees C).

5. Make a thin circle out of one dough ball on a floured surface while the oil is heating. Place a small amount of filling in the center, fold the dough into a half-moon shape, and seal the edges with your fingers. Fill and shape any additional empanadas as necessary.

6. Fry one to two empanadas at a time, in batches, for about 2 1/2 minutes per side or until browned. Dry off with paper towels—hot food.

39. Puff Pastry Shells

Prep Time: 10 minutes

Cook Time: 20 minutes

Total Time: 30 minutes

Servings: 4

Ingredients

- ➢ 1 egg, beaten
- ➢ 2 tbsp. water
- ➢ Four sheets of frozen puff pastry

Directions

1. In a small bowl, combine the water and the egg.
2. Create eight circles using a 3-inch round cutter by cutting two rounds from each puff pastry sheet. Four of the rounds should be cut with a two-1/2-inch round cutter. The uncut round should be placed on top of the entire cut round. Apply egg mixture to brush each.
3. Bake for 20 to 25 minutes or until puffed and golden in the preheated oven.

40. King Crab Appetizers

Prep Time: 10 minutes

Cook Time: 20 minutes

Total Time: 30 minutes

Servings: 12

Ingredients

- ➢ 2 (12 Oz.) packages of refrigerated biscuit dough
- ➢ 1 (8 Oz.) package of cream cheese, softened
- ➢ 1 (6 Oz.) can of crab meat, drained
- ➢ 2 tbsp. mayonnaise
- ➢ 2 tbsp. grated Parmesan cheese
- ➢ ½ cup of shredded Cheddar cheese
- ➢ 2 tbsp. thinly sliced green onion
- ➢ 1 tsp. Worcestershire sauce
- ➢ 1 pinch paprika

Directions

1. Three hundred seventy-five degrees Fahrenheit for baking (190 degrees C). Twelve tartlet pans should be lightly greased.
2. In the tartlet pans that have been prepared, press the divided rolls into the pans. Set a side.
3. In a large bowl, combine the cream cheese, crab, mayonnaise, Parmesan, Cheddar, green onions, and Worcestershire sauce. Each tart should contain 1 tsp. Add paprika on top of the mixture
4. At 375 degrees F, bake for 15 to 20 minutes or until golden brown (190 degrees C). Excellent for freezing; reheat before serving.

41. Easy Fried Eggplant

Prep Time: 20 minutes

Cook Time: 15 minutes

Total Time: 35 minutes

Servings: 4

Ingredients

- ➢ 2 tbsp. canola oil
- ➢ One large eggplant, peeled and sliced
- ➢ Three eggs, beaten
- ➢ 2 cups of dry bread crumbs

Directions

1. Over medium-high heat, preheat the oil in a big skillet.
2. Slices of eggplant are dipped in egg, then covered with breadcrumbs.
3. In hot oil, add breaded eggplant and cook for two to three minutes on each side or until golden brown. Dry off with paper towels.

42. Vegetarian Moussaka

Prep Time: 30 minutes

Cook Time: 1 hour 35 minutes

Additional Time: 30 minutes

Total Time: 2 hours 35 minutes

Servings: 8

Ingredients

- One eggplant, thinly sliced
- 1 tsp. salt, or more as needed
- 1 tbsp. olive oil, or more as needed
- One large zucchini, thinly sliced
- Two potatoes, thinly sliced
- One onion, sliced
- One clove of garlic, diced
- 1 tbsp. white vinegar
- 1 (14.5 Oz.) can of whole peeled tomatoes, diced
- ½ (14.5 Oz.) can of lentils, drained with liquid reserved
- 2 tbsp. diced fresh parsley
- 1 tsp. dried oregano
- ground black pepper to taste
- 1 cup of crumbled feta cheese

Sauce:

- One ¼ cup of milk
- 2 tbsp. all-purpose flour
- 1 ½ tbsp. butter
- One pinch of ground nutmeg
- ground black pepper to taste
- One large egg, beaten

Topping:

> ¼ cups of grated Parmesan cheese

Directions

1. Salt the slices of eggplant, then set them aside for 30 minutes. Use paper towels to dry after rinsing.
2. Set the oven to 375°F for preheating (190 degrees C).
3. A big skillet with medium-high heat is used to heat the olive oil. In hot oil, cook eggplant and zucchini on each side for three minutes or until lightly browned. Reserving as much oil as you can in the skillet, remove with a slotted spoon to drain on a plate lined with paper towels.
4. If necessary, fill the skillet with additional oil and heat it. Slices of potato should be browned after 3 to 5 minutes on each side in hot oil. With a slotted spoon, transfer to a plate lined with paper towels to drain, keeping the reserved oil in the skillet.
5. In the reserved oil, cook the onion and garlic for 5 to 7 minutes or until lightly browned. Add vinegar, bring to a boil, then reduce heat to medium-low and simmer for however long it takes for the liquid to thicken and reduce in volume. Add tomatoes, lentils, half of the lentil juice, parsley, and oregano. Put some salt and black pepper on it. Fifteen minutes of simmering are required. Cover, lower heat to medium-low.
6. In a 9x13-inch baking dish, distribute roughly 1/3 of the eggplant, zucchini, potatoes, and feta cheese. Repeat layering, ending with an eggplant and zucchini layer, and then pour half of the tomato mixture over the vegetables.
7. Bake for 25 minutes with a cover in a preheated oven.

8. Make the sauce while you wait. Whisk together the milk, flour, and butter; heat to a low boil, constantly stirring, until thick and smooth. Add black pepper and nutmeg for seasoning. After 5 minutes of cooling, remove from heat and add the beaten egg.

9. Add sauce to the vegetables before adding Parmesan cheese on top. Continue baking, uncovered, for another 25 to 30 minutes, or until the sauce bubbles and the top is lightly browned.

43.   Sheet Pan Roasted Vegetables

Prep Time: 30 minutes

Cook Time: 1 hour 30 minutes

Total Time: 2 hours

Servings: 24

Ingredients

➢ Eight zucchini, peeled and diced
➢ One eggplant, peeled and diced
➢ Eight carrots, diced
➢ 16 cherry tomatoes
➢ Two red onions, sliced
➢ One red bell pepper, sliced
➢ One yellow bell pepper, sliced
➢ ½ cup of olive oil
➢ 1 tsp. dried rosemary

- ➤ 1 tsp. dried thyme
- ➤ Two bay leaves, crushed
- ➤ 1 tsp. dried oregano
- ➤ Two cloves garlic, minced
- ➤ 2 tbsp. fresh lemon juice
- ➤ 1 tsp. grated lemon zest
- ➤ salt and pepper to taste

Directions

1. Blend the oil, rosemary, thyme, bay leaves, oregano, garlic, lemon juice, lemon zest, salt, and pepper with the zucchini, eggplant, carrots, tomatoes, onions, and peppers in a large bowl. Cover and refrigerate for at least two hours, preferably overnight.
2. Oven to 400 degrees Fahrenheit (200 degrees C).
3. The vegetables should be roasted for 20 minutes, uncovered, on a large roasting pan or until the tomatoes have split and some of the vegetables' edges are beginning to crisp. After removing and stirring it from the oven, put it back in for another 20 minutes. Turning the vegetables every 20 minutes, lower the heat to 200°F (95°C), and cook for 20 minutes or until tender.

44. Simple Artichoke Dip

Prep Time: 5 minutes

Cook Time: 20 minutes

Total Time: 25 minutes

Servings: 7

Ingredients

- ➤ One (14 Oz.) can of artichoke hearts, drained and diced
- ➤ 1 cup of mayonnaise
- ➤ 1 cup of grated Parmesan cheese

Directions

1. Set the oven to 375°F for preheating (190 degrees C).
2. Mayonnaise, Parmesan cheese, and artichoke hearts should all be thoroughly combined in a bowl. Fill a 9x13-inch baking dish with the mixture.
3. Bake for 15 to 20 minutes in a preheated oven or until bubbly and golden brown.

45. Grilled Garlic Artichokes

Prep Time: 5 minutes

Cook Time: 30 minutes

Total Time: 35 minutes

Servings: 4

Ingredients

- ➤ One lemon, quartered
- ➤ Two large artichokes
- ➤ ¾ cups of olive oil
- ➤ Four cloves garlic, diced
- ➤ 1 tsp. salt

- ➤ ½ tsp. ground black pepper

Directions

1. Large bowl with cold water in it. Add the juice of one wedge of lemon to the water. To keep artichokes from turning brown, trim the tops, then slice them in half lengthwise, placing the halves into the bowl of lemon water.
2. Bring a lot of water to a boil in a large pot. Set a grill outside to medium-high heat in the interim.
3. Artichokes should be cooked for about 15 minutes after being added to boiling water. Drain.
4. In a medium bowl, squeeze the remaining lemon wedges. Salt and pepper to taste, then stir in the garlic and olive oil.
5. Place the artichokes on the heated grill after brushing them with the garlic dip. Grill artichokes for 5 to 10 minutes, turning them frequently and basting with dip as you go.
6. With the remaining dip, serve right away.

46.   Eggplant Sandwiches

Prep Time: 20 minutes

Cook Time: 10 minutes

Total Time: 30 minutes

Servings: 2

Ingredients

- ➤ One small eggplant, halved and sliced
- ➤ 1 tbsp. olive oil, or as needed

- ➤ ¼ cups of mayonnaise
- ➤ Two cloves garlic, minced
- ➤ 2 (6-inch) French sandwich rolls
- ➤ One small tomato, sliced
- ➤ ½ cup of crumbled feta cheese
- ➤ ¼ cups of diced fresh basil leaves

Directions

1. Warm up the broiler in your oven. Arrange the sliced eggplant on a baking sheet or broiler pan after brushing them with olive oil. Remove the pan from the heat source by about 6 inches. Cook under the broiler for 10 minutes or until the food is toasty and tender.
2. French bread should be toast after being split lengthwise. Garlic and mayonnaise should be combined in a cup or small bowl. The toast should be covered with this mixture. Tomato, feta cheese, basil leaves, and slices of eggplant go inside the rolls.

47. Traditional Mexican Guacamole

Prep Time: 10 minutes

Total Time: 10 minutes

Servings: 4

Ingredients

- ➤ Two avocados, peeled and pitted
- ➤ 1 cup of diced tomatoes

- ¼ cups of diced onion
- ¼ cups of diced cilantro
- 2 tbsp. lemon juice
- One jalapeno pepper, seeded and minced
- salt and ground black pepper to taste

Directions

1. To make avocados creamy, mash them in a bowl.
2. Combine the mashed avocado with the tomatoes, onion, cilantro, lemon juice, and jalapeno pepper thoroughly. Add pepper and salt to taste.

48. Artichoke Hearts Gratin

Prep Time: 10 minutes

Cook Time: 10 minutes

Additional Time: 15 minutes

Total Time: 35 minutes

Servings: 4

Ingredients

- Six canned artichoke hearts drained and halved
- 1 tsp. vegetable oil
- salt and freshly ground black pepper to taste
- 2 tbsp. dry bread crumbs
- ¼ cups of finely grated Parmigiano-Reggiano cheese
- 1 tbsp. olive oil

> ➢ ½ lemon, cut into wedges

Directions

1. Half an artichoke heart should be cut down on a paper towel to drain for about 15 minutes.
2. Set the broiler high and place the oven rack about 6 inches from the heat source. Aluminum foil should be used to line a baking sheet. Vegetable oil should be used sparingly.
3. Cut side up, and place the artichoke heart halves on the prepared baking sheet. Add pepper and salt to taste. Olive oil should be drizzled after the cheese has been topped with breadcrumbs.
4. Artichoke hearts should be browned on top after about 7 minutes of broiling. Lemon wedges are optional.

49. Roasted Artichokes

Prep Time: 5 minutes

Cook Time: 1 hour 20 minutes

Total Time: 1 hour 25 minutes

Servings: 4

Ingredients

> ➢ Four large whole artichokes, top 1 inch and stems removed
> ➢ ¼ cups of fresh lemon juice
> ➢ ¼ cups of olive oil
> ➢ Four cloves garlic, cloves peeled and crushed
> ➢ kosher salt

Directions

1. Oven: 425 degrees Fahrenheit (220 degrees C).
2. Put the artichokes in a bowl stem-side down and add lemon juice.
3. With your hands, loosen the artichoke leaves slightly. To make a space the size of a garlic clove, insert a knife blade into the center of each artichoke.
4. One garlic clove should be pressed into the center of each artichoke before adding salt and a drizzle of olive oil.
5. Each artichoke should be double-wrapped in heavy-duty aluminum foil and placed in a baking dish.
6. Bake for about one hour and 20 minutes in a preheated oven or until sizzling.

50. Instant Pot Steamed Artichokes

Prep Time: 5 minutes

Cook Time: 20 minutes

Additional Time: 5 minutes

Total Time: 30 minutes

Servings: 4

Ingredients

➢ 1 cup of water
➢ Two cloves garlic
➢ One bay leaf
➢ ½ tsp. salt

> Four artichokes, trimmed and stemmed
> 2 tbsp. lemon juice

Directions

1. In a multipurpose pressure cooker (like the Instant Pot®), combine the water, garlic, bay leaf, and salt. Set the steamer inside the pot. Add artichokes and trimmings facing up, and squeeze some lemon juice over them. Shut and secure the lid. Set the timer for 10 minutes and choose high pressure as the manufacturer directs. The pressure should build for 10 to 15 minutes.
2. Use the quick-release technique cautiously and follow the manufacturer's instructions for about 5 minutes. Dispatch the lock and lid.
3. Allow cooling until manageable. One at a time, remove the outer petals. Pull the soft part of the petal out with your teeth. Delete the last petal. Toss the fuzzy center that is close to the stem. Consume the bottom whole or in pieces.

51. Roquefort Pear Salad

Prep Time: 25 minutes

Cook Time: 10 minutes

Total Time: 35 minutes

Servings: 6

Ingredients
Caramelized Pecans:

- ½ cup of pecans

¼ cups of white sugar

Mustard Vinaigrette:

- ⅓ cups of olive oil
- 3 tbsp. red wine vinegar
- 1 ½ tsp. white sugar
- 1 ½ tsp. prepared mustard
- One clove of garlic, diced
- ½ tsp. salt
- fresh ground black pepper to taste

Salad:

- One head of green leaf lettuce torn into bite-sized pieces
- Three medium pears - peeled, cored, and diced
- 5 Oz. Roquefort cheese, crumbled
- One medium avocado - peeled, pitted, and diced
- ½ cup of thinly sliced green onions

Directions

1. Making the pecans is as simple as mixing sugar and pecans in a skillet over medium heat. Cook for 5 to 7 minutes, occasionally stirring, until the sugar has melted and the pecans are caramelized. Transfer the nuts carefully to a piece of wax paper to cool.
2. Prepare the dressing while the nuts cool. Combine the salt, sugar, mustard, garlic, vinegar, oil, and pepper in a bowl.
3. Build the salad: In a big serving bowl, arrange lettuce, pears, avocado, Roquefort cheese, and green onions. Dress the top with dressing.

4. Pecans that have cooled should be broken up and sprinkled over the salad.

52.   Paleo Baked Eggs in Avocado

Prep Time: 10 minutes

Cook Time: 15 minutes

Total Time: 25 minutes

Servings: 2

Ingredients

- ➤ Two small eggs
- ➤ One avocado halved and pitted
- ➤ 2 tsp. diced fresh chives, or to taste
- ➤ One pinch of dried parsley, or to taste
- ➤ One pinch of sea salt and ground black pepper to taste
- ➤ Two slices of cooked bacon, crumbled

Directions

1. Oven: 425 degrees Fahrenheit (220 degrees C).
2. With care to preserve the yolks, crack eggs into a bowl.
3. Place the halves of the avocado in a baking dish, resting them along the edge to prevent them from toppling. In the avocado hole, carefully spoon one egg yolk. Fill the hole with egg white by spoonfuls until it is full. Continue with the remaining avocado, egg white, and yolk. Chives, parsley, sea salt, and pepper should be used to season each filled avocado.

4. Bake the eggs in the baking dish for about 15 minutes, gently placing them in the oven. Over avocado, top with bacon.

53. Buttery Garlic Green Beans

Prep Time: 5 minutes

Cook Time: 10 minutes

Total Time: 15 minutes

Servings: 4

Ingredients

➤ 1 lb fresh green beans, trimmed and snapped in half
➤ 3 tbsp. butter
➤ Three cloves garlic, minced
➤ ⅛ tsp. lemon-pepper seasoning, or more to taste
➤ salt to taste

Directions

1. In a big skillet, add the green beans and cover with water. Bring to a boil. Reduce heat to medium-low, cover, and simmer for 3 to 5 minutes or until beans soften.
2. Drain again, then add to skillet. Melt the butter by adding it and stirring for 1 to 2 minutes.
3. Add the garlic and cook for one to two minutes, until it is fragrant and soft.
4. Salt and lemon-pepper seasoning should be added before serving.

54. Crisp Pickled Green Beans

Prep Time: 15 minutes

Cook Time: 20 minutes

Additional Time: 14 days, 8 hours

Total Time: 14 days, 8 hours 35 minutes

Servings: 48

Ingredients

- 2 ½ cups of distilled white vinegar
- 2 cups of water
- ¼ cups of salt
- One clove of garlic, peeled
- 2 ½ lbs fresh green beans
- Six large sprigs of dill
- ¾ tsp. red pepper flakes

Directions

1. Check six 1/2-pint jars for rust and cracks, and discard any damaged ones. Put into simmering water. Warm soapy water should be used to wash new, unused lids and rings.
2. Stir the vinegar, water, and salt in a big saucepan while sterilizing the jars. Add the garlic and heat the mixture until it is boiling vigorously.
3. Green beans should be trimmed to be 1/4 inch shorter than the jars.

4. Jars from the simmering water. Add one dill sprig and one-eighth tsp. of red pepper flakes to each jar. Add green beans that are standing on end.

5. Pour boiling brine into the jars, filling them to within 1/4 inch of the tops (omitting the garlic). Using rings and lids, secure jars.

6. A large stockpot should have a rack in the bottom, and the water should be half full. Using a holder, bring to a boil before dropping the jars 2 inches apart. Add more boiling water to the pot to cover the jars by at least an inch. Simmer for 10 minutes with a lid on, taking care not to boil.

7. After cooling for 8 to 12 hours, remove the jars from the stockpot. By gently pressing on the center of the lid, you can check a jar's seal; it shouldn't budge.

8. Before eating, allow green beans to ferment in a cool, dark area for two to three weeks.

9. Eat the beans within a week if the jars don't properly seal.

55. Quick and Easy Vegetable Soup

Prep Time: 15 minutes

Cook Time: 35 minutes

Total Time: 50 minutes

Servings: 6

Ingredients
➢ 1 (14.5 Oz.) can dice tomatoes

- 1 (14 Oz.) can of chicken broth
- 1 (11.5 Oz.) can tomato-vegetable juice cocktail
- Two carrots, sliced
- Two stalks of celery, diced
- One large potato, diced
- 1 cup of diced fresh green beans
- 1 cup of fresh corn kernels
- 1 cup of water
- salt and pepper to taste
- One pinch of Creole seasoning, or more to taste

Directions

1. Amass all the ingredients.
2. A sizable stockpot should be filled with water, carrots, celery, potatoes, green beans, tomatoes, chicken broth, and juice. Add Creole seasoning, salt, and pepper to taste.
3. Cook for 30 minutes or until vegetables are tender after bringing to a boil over medium heat.

56. Smothered Green Beans

Prep Time: 20 minutes

Cook Time: 30 minutes

Total Time: 50 minutes

Servings: 6

Ingredients

- Six thick slices of bacon, diced

- ½ cup of onions, minced
- 1 tsp. minced garlic
- 1 lb fresh green beans, trimmed
- 1 cup of water, or as needed
- ⅛ tsp. salt
- One pinch of ground black pepper

Directions

1. Bacon should be cooked until fat renders in a sizable, deep skillet over medium-high heat. Cook and stir for a minute after adding the onion and garlic.
2. Water and beans are combined. Cook beans until they are tender and all water has been absorbed. Till the beans are tender, gradually add more water. Add pepper and salt to taste.

57. Stuffed Cream Cheese Mushrooms

Prep Time: 15 minutes

Cook Time: 25 minutes

Additional Time: 10 minutes

Total Time: 50 minutes

Servings: 6

Ingredients

- cooking spray
- 12 whole fresh mushrooms, tough ends trimmed

- ➤ 1 tbsp. vegetable oil
- ➤ 1 tbsp. minced garlic
- ➤ 1 (8 Oz.) package of cream cheese, softened
- ➤ ¼ cups of grated Parmesan cheese
- ➤ ¼ tsp. ground black pepper
- ➤ ¼ tsp. onion powder
- ➤ ¼ tsp. cayenne pepper

Directions

1. Oven: 350 degrees Fahrenheit (175 degrees C). Apply cooking spray to a baking sheet.
2. Use a damp paper towel to clean the mushrooms. Mushroom stems should be carefully broken. Finely chop stems and reserve caps.
3. Over medium heat, warm oil in a big skillet. Garlic should not be burned while cooking diced mushroom stems in hot oil for 3 to 5 minutes or until moisture evaporates. After 10 minutes, spread the mushroom mixture into a bowl to finish cooling.
4. The cooled mushroom mixture should be thoroughly combined and thickened by adding cream cheese, Parmesan cheese, black pepper, onion powder, and cayenne pepper. Use a small spoon to place a generous amount of stuffing inside each mushroom cap. On the cookie sheet that has been prepared, arrange the stuffed mushrooms.
5. Bake in the preheated oven for about 20 minutes or until each cap is dripping with liquid.

58. Hearty Vegetable Lasagna

Prep Time: 25 minutes

Cook Time: 1 hour

Additional Time: 15 minutes

Total Time: 1 hour 40 minutes

Servings: 12

Ingredients

- 1 (16 Oz.) package of lasagna noodles
- 2 tbsp. vegetable oil
- 1 lb fresh mushrooms, sliced
- ¾ cups of diced green bell pepper
- ¾ cups of diced onion
- Three cloves garlic, minced
- 2 (26 Oz.) jars of pasta sauce
- 1 tsp. dried basil
- 1 (15 Oz.) container part-skim ricotta cheese
- 4 cups of shredded mozzarella cheese, divided
- Two eggs
- ½ cup of grated Parmesan cheese

Directions

1. For 10 minutes, or until al dente, cook lasagna noodles in a big pot of boiling water. Drain the rinse after using cold water.
2. Oil is heated in a big pot. Cook and stir the mushrooms, green peppers, onion, and garlic for about 5 minutes or until

tender. Bring to a boil while stirring in the basil pasta sauce—15 minutes of simmering after lowering the heat.

3. Ricotta, 2 cups of mozzarella cheese, and eggs should all be combined in a medium bowl while the sauce is simmering.
4. Oven: 350 degrees Fahrenheit (175 degrees C). Clean and grease a 9x13-inch baking pan.
5. The bottom of the baking dish should be covered with 1 cup of cooked tomato and vegetable sauce. Lay out half the lasagna noodles, then top with half the ricotta mixture, sauce, and Parmesan cheese. Layer the noodles, ricotta mixture, sauce, and Parmesan cheese again. Finish with the final 2 cups of mozzarella.
6. Forty minutes of uncovered baking are required in the preheated oven. Before serving, let stand for 15 minutes.

59. Air-Fryer Roasted Veggies

Prep Time: 20 minutes

Cook Time: 10 minutes

Total Time: 30 minutes

Servings: 4

Ingredients
- ½ cup of diced zucchini
- ½ cup of diced summer squash
- ½ cup of diced mushrooms
- ½ cup of diced cauliflower

- ½ cup of diced asparagus
- ½ cup of diced sweet red pepper
- 2 tsp. vegetable oil
- ¼ tsp. salt
- ¼ tsp. ground black pepper
- 1/4 tsp. seasoning, or more to taste

Directions

1. Amass all the ingredients.
2. Set the air fryer to 360°F before using it (180 degrees C).
3. In a big bowl, mix the zucchini, squash, mushrooms, cauliflower, asparagus, red pepper, oil, salt, pepper, and other seasonings as desired. Arrange in a single layer in the fryer basket after tossing to coat.
4. Cook in the preheated air fryer, stirring once halfway through, for 10 minutes or until tender-crisp.

60. Microwave Baked Potato

Prep Time: 1 minute

Cook Time: 11 minutes

Total Time: 12 minutes

Servings: 1

Ingredients

- One large russet potato
- salt and ground black pepper to taste
- 1 tbsp. butter

> 2 tbsp. shredded Cheddar cheese
> 1 tbsp. sour cream

Directions

1. Amass all the ingredients.
2. Potato with a brush and a fork. Put on a plate that can be used in a microwave.
3. Five minutes of full-power microwave cooking. The potato should be microwaved for an additional five minutes or until soft.
4. After taking the potato out of the microwave, cut it in half lengthwise. Sprinkle with salt and pepper and slightly smash the interior with a fork.
5. Combine Cheddar cheese and butter. About one more minute of microwaving will melt the food.
6. Serve with sour cream on top.

Chapter 4: Fish and Seafood

61. Gochujang Honey Shrimp

Prep Time: 10 minutes

Cook Time: 5 minutes

Total Time: 15 minutes

Servings: 4

Ingredients

- 16 Oz. uncooked medium shrimp, peeled and deveined
- garlic powder to taste
- , salt to taste
- 3 tbsp. gochujang, or to taste
- 2 tbsp. honey
- 1 tbsp. sesame oil
- 3 tsp. soy sauce
- 1 tsp. freshly squeezed lemon juice
- Three cloves garlic, minced
- 1 tsp. minced fresh ginger root
- 1 ½ tbsp. vegetable oil, or more as needed
- ½ cup of water
- 1 tsp. cornstarch
- 1 tsp. sesame seeds
- scallions, sliced diagonally, as a garnish

Directions

1. Garlic powder and salt should be used to season the shrimp on both sides.
2. Gochujang, honey, sesame oil, soy sauce, lemon juice, garlic, and ginger should all be thoroughly mixed in a bowl. Set apart.
3. Over medium-high heat, preheat the oil in a nonstick skillet. Add the shrimp and cook for 2 to 3 minutes, flipping halfway through, until the meat is opaque and the outside is bright pink. Take your time. The pan, and take the shrimp out.
4. Lower the heat to low and stir in the sauce in the skillet. A slurry is created by combining water and cornstarch in a small bowl. Mix the slurry thoroughly with the sauce. For

about a minute, cook while constantly stirring until the sauce thickens slightly. Stirring until coated and barely heated through, add shrimp back to the skillet.

5. Add scallions and sesame seeds as a garnish—hot food.

62.   Sheet Pan Cajun Butter Shrimp

Prep Time: 15 minutes

Cook Time: 8 minutes

Total Time: 23 minutes

Servings: 6

Ingredients
Cajun Seasoning

- ➢ 1 tsp. smoked paprika
- ➢ ½ tsp. garlic powder
- ➢ ½ tsp. onion powder
- ➢ ½ tsp. salt
- ➢ ½ tsp. dried oregano
- ➢ ¼ tsp. freshly ground black pepper
- ➢ ¼ tsp. cayenne pepper
- ➢ ¼ tsp. dried thyme

Shrimp

- ➢ Two lbs extra large shrimp, peeled and deveined
- ➢ 2 tbsp. olive oil
- ➢ ½ cups of butter, cubed and at room temperature

- ➢ 2 tbsp. minced fresh parsley
- ➢ Six lemon wedges

Directions

1. Oven: 400 degrees Fahrenheit (200 degrees C).
2. Mix smoked paprika, garlic powder, onion powder, salt, oregano, pepper, cayenne, and thyme in a small bowl. Put the shrimp in a big bowl after drying them off. Olive oil should be drizzled over the Cajun seasoning mixture. Evenly coat with a toss.
3. Without crowding the pan, arrange the shrimp in a single layer.
4. For about 8 minutes in a preheated oven, cook shrimp until the middles are opaque. When the butter is added, toss in the shrimp and cook until the butter is melted. Serve with lemon wedges and, if desired, a sprinkle of parsley.

63. Air Fryer Tilapia

Prep Time: 5 minutes

Cook Time: 6 minutes

Total Time: 11 minutes

Servings: 4

Ingredients

- ➢ ½ cup of freshly grated Parmesan cheese
- ➢ 1 ½ tsp. paprika
- ➢ 1 tsp. garlic powder

- ½ tsp. salt
- ½ tsp. freshly ground black pepper
- 4 (6 Oz.) tilapia fillets, thawed if frozen
- cooking spray
- 1 tbsp. minced fresh parsley
- Four lemon wedges

Directions

1. 400°F should be the preheated temperature of the air fryer (200 degrees C).
2. Combine the parmesan cheese, paprika, garlic powder, salt, and pepper in a bowl.
3. Tilapia filets should be dried with paper towels. Spray the fillets on both sides with cooking spray before pressing them into the Parmesan mixture. Spray some more cooking spray after shaking off any extra. Insert in the air fryer's basket.
4. 6 to 8 minutes of cooking time should be enough for the fish to flake easily. Depending on the size of your air fryer, it might be necessary to cook the fish in two batches.
5. Serve with lemon wedges and a parsley garnish.

64. Grilled Garlic Shrimp

Prep Time: 15 minutes

Cook Time: 6 minutes

Marinate Time: 30 minutes

Total Time: 51 minutes

Servings: 4

Ingredients

- ➤ 3 tbsp. olive oil
- ➤ 1 tbsp. lemon juice
- ➤ Three cloves garlic, minced
- ➤ 1 tbsp. minced fresh parsley
- ➤ 1 tbsp. minced fresh basil
- ➤ ½ tsp. garlic salt
- ➤ ⅛ tsp. freshly ground black pepper
- ➤ One lb extra large shrimp, peeled and deveined
- ➤ Six wooden skewers

Directions

The oil, lemon juice, garlic cloves, parsley, basil, garlic, salt, and pepper should all be combined in a food processor's bowl. Blend the marinade until it is smooth, for about 20 seconds.

Fill a plastic bag that can seal a gallon with the marinade. Toss the prawn in the marinade and add them to the bag. Place the bag in the refrigerator for 30 minutes after sealing.

While the prawn is marinating, soak wooden skewers in cold water.

Set an outdoor grill to high heat and quickly oil the grates.

After being removed from the marinade, five to six prawns should be threaded onto each skewer. About 3 minutes per side, grill the prawn on the preheated grill until they are bright pink on the outside and opaque in the center.

65.   Proper British Fish Cakes

Prep Time: 15 minutes

Cook Time: 20 minutes

Additional Time: 15 minutes

Total Time: 50 minutes

Servings: 4

Ingredients
For the Tartar Sauce:

- ½ cup of mayonnaise
- 2 tbsp. capers, drained and diced
- 1 tbsp. finely diced shallot
- 1 tbsp. finely diced Italian parsley
- 1 tbsp. finely diced fresh tarragon
- 2 tsp. prepared horseradish
- 1 tsp. Dijon mustard
- One pinch of cayenne pepper

For the Fish Cakes:

- ½ cup of milk
- One bay leaf
- 1 lb cod, cut into 1-inch pieces
- salt and freshly ground black pepper to taste
- 12 Oz. russet potato, peeled and quartered
- One pinch of cayenne pepper

- ➤ 1 tbsp. finely diced Italian parsley
- ➤ 1 tbsp. sliced fresh chives
- ➤ 1 tsp. Finely grated lemon zest

For the Breading:

- ➤ ⅓ cups of all-purpose flour
- ➤ One large egg, beaten
- ➤ 1 cup of panko bread crumbs, or as needed
- ➤ ¼ cups of vegetable oil, or as needed

Directions

1. Refrigerate tartar sauce until required by combining mayonnaise, capers, shallot, parsley, tarragon, horseradish, mustard, and cayenne in a bowl.
2. The fish pieces should be placed in a saucepan on top of the milk and bay leaf. Add salt to the dish. Stirring occasionally, simmer over medium heat for about a minute. Remove the fish from the heat and cover it as soon as it firms up before it flakes apart. Prior to draining, let sit for five minutes. Allow 10 minutes for cooling. Until needed, keep chilled.
3. In the interim, scald a pot of lightly salted water. Boil the russet potato until it is tender but still holds together.
4. Drain the potato and mash it in a bowl. Add salt, black pepper, and cayenne to season. Add the chives, parsley, and lemon zest after adding 1 tbsp of the tartar sauce mixture. Blend thoroughly. Fish flake chilled over top. Blend thoroughly.
5. 1/4 of the mixture should be taken and formed into a patty. Continue with the remaining mixture.

6. Cakes are dusted with flour on both sides. Cakes should be egg-brushed on both sides. Add bread crumbs to coat.

7. Over medium heat, warm the oil in a skillet. Patties should be fried in hot oil for 3 to 4 minutes per side or until golden brown and thoroughly heated; before serving with tartar sauce, drain on paper towels.

66. Maple Mustard Salmon

Prep Time: 10 minutes

Cook Time: 10 minutes

Total Time: 20 minutes

Servings: 6

Ingredients

- 2 ½ tbsp. stone-ground mustard
- 1 tbsp. maple syrup
- 1 tsp. Fresh lemon juice
- ½ tsp. minced garlic
- ¼ tsp. minced fresh thyme
- 6 (6 Oz.) frozen salmon fillets, thawed and patted dry
- 1 tsp. kosher salt
- ½ tsp. black pepper
- 1 tbsp. olive oil

Directions

1. Oven: 400 degrees Fahrenheit (200 degrees C). A big baking sheet should be foil-lined.

2. Combine the thyme, maple syrup, lemon juice, mustard, and mustard in a small bowl.
3. Salmon should be seasoned with salt and pepper and brushed with oil on both sides. Place the salmon on the prepared baking sheet. Apply the mustard mixture to a brush.
4. Bake in the oven for 8 to 10 minutes or until the salmon flakes easily with a fork.

67. Seafood Pot Pie

Prep Time: 30 minutes

Cook Time: 1 hour

Rest Time: 10 minutes

Total Time: 1 hour 40 minutes

Servings: 6

Ingredients

- ½ cup of unsalted butter
- 1 ½ cups of thinly sliced yellow onion
- 1 cup of thinly sliced fennel
- 1 cup of thinly sliced celery
- 1 cup of thinly sliced carrots
- ½ cup of all-purpose flour
- ½ cup of dry white wine
- 3 cups of fish stock
- ¼ cups of heavy cream, divided

- ➢ 1 tbsp. kosher salt
- ➢ ½ tsp. ground black pepper
- ➢ 1 (8 Oz.) fillet halibut, skin removed, cut into 1-inch pieces
- ➢ ½ lb sea scallops halved horizontally
- ➢ ½ lb peeled and deveined medium shrimp
- ➢ 1 lb jumbo lump crabmeat, picked over
- ➢ 1 cup of frozen green peas
- ➢ 2 tbsp. diced fresh parsley, plus more for garnish
- ➢ One large egg, lightly beaten
- ➢ 1 (17.3 Oz.) package of frozen puff pastry sheets, thawed

Directions

1. Over medium-high heat, melt the butter in a sizable pan. Add the vegetables: onion, fennel, celery, and carrots; cook for about 8 minutes, stirring frequently, until the vegetables are softened, and the onion is translucent. For one minute, thoroughly coat the vegetables with flour after adding them. Stir in the wine for about 15 seconds or until the wine has completely evaporated. Add 3 tbsp. Stir the mixture of cream and the fish stock for about 5 minutes or until it thickens into a creamy sauce. Seafood, green peas, and parsley are gently folded after seasoning with salt and pepper.

2. Turn down the heat to medium-low, gently stir the mixture frequently, and cook for 6 to 8 minutes, or until the sauce is warmed through but the seafood is still slightly raw in the middle. 5 (18 to 20 Oz.) ramekins or oven-safe bowls should each have 2 cups of mixture added to them. Put the bowls on a rimmed baking sheet covered with foil.

3. Three hundred seventy-five degrees Fahrenheit for baking (190 degrees C). Install the middle oven rack.

4. Combine the remaining 1 tbsp of heavy cream in a small bowl with the egg. Defrosted puff pastry sheets should be placed on a lightly dusted work surface. Cut each square into quarters after rolling each sheet into a 13" x 13" square. Throw away any extra pastries. A square of pastry should be placed on top of each bowl, with the corners folded artistically to fit the shape of the bowl. To allow steam to escape while baking, cut three tiny slits in the center of the pastry using the tip of a knife. The top of the pastry can be garnished with diced parsley or fennel fronds. Eggwash should be used to press the garnishes onto the pastry lightly.

5. Bake the individual portions on a baking sheet in the oven for about 40 minutes or until the pastry is golden brown and the filling is hot and bubbling. Before serving, allow cooling for ten minutes.

68. Gochujang Glazed Salmon

Prep Time: 5 minutes

Cook Time: 20 minutes

Total Time: 25 minutes

Servings: 2

Ingredients

- ➤ 8 Oz. salmon fillets
- ➤ 1 tbsp. gochujang
- ➤ 2 tbsp. pineapple juice
- ➤ One pinch of black sesame seeds
- ➤ One pinch of white sesame seeds
- ➤ 1 tbsp. sliced green onions, or to taste

Directions

1. Oven: 350 degrees Fahrenheit (175 degrees C)
2. Combine the pineapple juice and gochujang in a small bowl to produce a glaze. Place salmon on a baking sheet and brush with mixture.
3. About 20 minutes into baking, the salmon should easily flake with a fork.
4. Green onion and sesame seeds can be added to salmon.

69.   Good New Orleans Creole Gumbo

Prep Time: 1 hour

Cook Time: 2 hours 40 minutes

Total Time: 3 hours 40 minutes

Servings: 20

Ingredients

- ➤ 1 cup of all-purpose flour
- ➤ ¾ cups of bacon drippings
- ➤ 1 cup of coarsely diced celery

- ➢ One large onion, coarsely diced
- ➢ One large green bell pepper, coarsely diced
- ➢ Two cloves garlic, minced
- ➢ 1 lb andouille sausage, sliced
- ➢ 3 quarts water
- ➢ 6 cubes beef bouillon
- ➢ 1 tbsp. white sugar
- ➢ salt to taste
- ➢ 2 tbsp. hot pepper sauce, or to taste
- ➢ ½ tsp. Cajun seasoning blend, or to taste
- ➢ Four bay leaves
- ➢ ½ tsp. dried thyme leaves
- ➢ 1 (14.5 Oz.) can of stewed tomatoes
- ➢ 1 (6 Oz.) can of tomato sauce
- ➢ Four tsp. file powder, divided
- ➢ 2 tbsp. bacon drippings
- ➢ 2 (10 Oz.) packages of frozen cut okra, thawed
- ➢ 2 tbsp. distilled white vinegar
- ➢ 1 lb lump crabmeat
- ➢ 3 lbs uncooked medium shrimp, peeled and deveined
- ➢ 2 tbsp. Worcestershire sauce

Directions

1. Amass all the ingredients.
2. Build the roux: In a sizable, heavy saucepan over medium-low heat, combine flour and 3/4 cups of bacon drippings and whisk until smooth. Cook the roux while continuously whisking it until it turns deep mahogany brown. This could take 20 to 30 minutes; whisk continuously and watch the

heat closely to prevent burning. Whisk the mixture until cooking stops, then turn off the heat.

3. Build the gumbo: To make very finely diced vegetables, add celery, onion, green bell pepper, and garlic to the work bowl of a food processor.

4. The roux should be mixed with the sausage and vegetables. Cook the mixture for 10 to 15 minutes, or until vegetables are fork-tender, at a simmer over medium-low heat. Remove from the heat and reserve.

5. Over medium-high heat, bring water and beef bouillon cubes to a boil in a big Dutch oven or soup pot. Whisk the roux mixture into the boiling water when the bouillon cubes are completely dissolved.

6. Add sugar, salt, hot sauce, Cajun seasoning, bay leaves, thyme, stewed tomatoes, and tomato sauce after lowering the heat to a simmer. 2 tsp. of file gumbo powder should be added at the 45-minute mark of the soup's 1-hour simmering period.

7. On medium heat, melt 2 tbsp of bacon drippings in a skillet. Okra and vinegar are added, cooked for 15 minutes, then removed with a slotted spoon and stirred into the gumbo that is currently simmering.

8. Stir in the Worcestershire sauce, crabmeat, and shrimp, set aside, and simmer for 45 minutes to blend the flavors. Just before serving, stir in 2 additional tsp of file gumbo powder.

70. Vietnamese Fresh Spring Rolls

Prep Time: 45 minutes

Cook Time: 5 minutes

Total Time: 50 minutes

Servings: 8

Ingredients

- 2 Oz. rice vermicelli
- Eight rice wrappers (8.5-inch diameter)
- Eight large cooked shrimp - peeled, deveined, and cut in half
- Two leaves of lettuce, diced
- 3 tbsp. diced fresh mint leaves
- 3 tbsp. diced fresh cilantro
- One ⅓ tbsp. diced fresh Thai basil

Sauces:

- ¼ cups of water
- 2 tbsp. fresh lime juice
- 2 tbsp. white sugar
- 4 tsp. fish sauce
- One clove of garlic, minced
- ½ tsp. garlic chili sauce
- 3 tbsp. hoisin sauce
- 1 tsp. Finely diced peanuts

Directions

1. Vermicelli pasta should be added after the water in a large pot has been lightly salted and brought to a rolling boil.

Pasta should be cooked uncovered for 3 to 5 minutes while occasionally stirring to keep it firm to the bite.

2. Warm water should be added to a big bowl. One wrapper should be placed in hot water for one second to soften. Spread the wrapper flat and arrange two shrimp halves in a row down the middle. Next, add some vermicelli, lettuce, mint, cilantro, and basil, leaving about 2 inches uncovered on each side. Roll the wrapper tightly, starting with the lettuce at the end and folding the uncovered sides inward. Apply the remaining ingredients again.

3. As for the sauces: In a small bowl, thoroughly combine the following ingredients: water, lime juice, sugar, fish sauce, garlic, and chili sauce. In a separate tiny bowl, combine the peanuts and hoisin sauce.

4. Serve the rolled spring rolls with fish sauce and hoisin sauce.

71. Shrimp Scampi with Pasta

Prep Time: 20 minutes

Cook Time: 20 minutes

Total Time: 40 minutes

Servings: 6

Ingredients

➢ 1 (16 Oz.) package of linguine pasta
➢ 2 tbsp. butter

- ➢ 2 tbsp. extra-virgin olive oil
- ➢ Two shallots, finely diced
- ➢ Two cloves garlic, minced
- ➢ 1 pinch red pepper flakes
- ➢ 1 lb shrimp, peeled and deveined
- ➢ One pinch of kosher salt and freshly ground pepper
- ➢ ½ cup of dry white wine
- ➢ One lemon, juiced
- ➢ 2 tbsp. butter
- ➢ 2 tbsp. extra-virgin olive oil
- ➢ ¼ cups of finely diced fresh parsley leaves
- ➢ 1 tsp. extra-virgin olive oil, or to taste

Directions

1. Ingredient gathering.
2. Linguine should be cooked in boiling, salted water for 6 to 8 minutes or until almost tender. Drain.
3. Over medium heat, melt 2 tbsp. Of butter and 2 tbsp. Of olive oil in a big skillet.
4. The hot butter and oil should cook and stir the shallots, garlic, and red pepper flakes for 3 to 4 minutes or until the shallots are translucent.
5. Add the prawn to the skillet, season with kosher salt and black pepper, and cook for 2 to 3 minutes, occasionally stirring, until pink. The prawn in the skillet can be saved for later.
6. White wine and lemon juice should be added to the skillet. While cooking, use a wooden spoon to scrape up any browned food bits from the bottom of the pan.

7. 2 tbsp. Of butter should be melted in a skillet. 2 tbsp. Olive oil should be added, and the mixture should be simmered.
8. Season the linguine, shrimp, and parsley with salt and black pepper and toss to combine. Add 1 tsp. Of olive oil before serving.

72. Best Tuna Casserole

Prep Time: 10 minutes

Cook Time: 20 minutes

Total Time: 30 minutes

Servings: 6

Ingredients

➢ 1 (12 Oz.) package of egg noodles
➢ Two (10.5 Oz.) cans of condensed cream of mushroom soup
➢ 2 cups of shredded Cheddar cheese, divided
➢ 2 (5 Oz.) cans tuna, drained
➢ 1 cup of frozen green peas
➢ ½ (4.5 Oz.) can of sliced mushrooms
➢ ¼ cups of diced onion
➢ 1 cup of crushed potato chips

Directions

1. Amass all the ingredients.
2. Lightly salt the water in a big pot, then quickly bring it to a boil. Cook egg noodles at a boil for 7 to 9 minutes or until tender but firm to the bite.

3. In the interim, heat the oven to 425 degrees F. (220 degrees C).
4. Noodles, condensed soup, 1 cup of cheese, tuna, peas, mushrooms, and onion should all be thoroughly mixed in a large bowl.
5. Fill a 9x13-inch baking dish with the mixture.
6. Add 1 cup of cheese and crushed potato chip to the mixture.
7. Bake in a preheated oven for 15 to 20 minutes or until the cheese is bubbly.

73. Marinated Tuna Steak

Prep Time: 10 minutes

Cook Time: 10 minutes

Additional Time: 30 minutes

Total Time: 50 minutes

Servings: 4

Ingredients

- ¼ cups of orange juice
- ¼ cups of soy sauce
- 2 tbsp. olive oil
- 2 tbsp. diced fresh parsley
- 1 tbsp. lemon juice
- One clove of garlic, minced
- ½ tsp. diced fresh oregano
- ½ tsp. ground black pepper

➢ 4 (4 Oz.) tuna steaks

Directions

1. In a sizable non-reactive dish, thoroughly combine the following ingredients: orange juice, soy sauce, olive oil, parsley, lemon juice, garlic, oregano, and pepper. Turn the tuna steaks to coat with the marinade. The dish should marinate in the fridge for at least 30 minutes while wrapped in plastic.
2. High heat should be set on an outdoor grill before lightly oiling the grates. Remove the tuna steaks from the marinade, shaking off the extra and saving the marinade for basting.
3. On a preheated grill, cook tuna steaks for 5 to 6 minutes before flipping them over and basting them with the reserved marinade. Continue to cook for an additional 5 minutes or until the desired doneness. Delete any leftover marinade.

74. Grilled Salmon

Prep Time: 15 minutes

Cook Time: 16 minutes

Additional Time: 2 hours

Total Time: 2 hours 31 minutes

Servings: 6

Ingredients

- ➢ 1 ½ lbs salmon fillets
- ➢ lemon pepper to taste
- ➢ garlic powder to taste
- ➢ salt to taste
- ➢ ⅓ cups of soy sauce
- ➢ ⅓ cups of brown sugar
- ➢ ⅓ cups of water
- ➢ ¼ cups of vegetable oil

Directions

1. Salt, pepper, and garlic powder are used to season salmon fillets.
2. Stir the soy sauce, brown sugar, water, and vegetable oil in a small bowl until the sugar is dissolved. Put the fish in a sizable plastic bag that can be sealed, add the soy sauce mixture, and turn to coat. For at least two hours, refrigerate.
3. Fire up the grill to medium heat.
4. Grill grate with a little oil. Discard the marinade before placing the salmon on the hot grill. For salmon, cook for 6 to 8 minutes on each side or until the fish flakes easily.

75. Perfect Ten Baked Cod

Prep Time: 10 minutes

Cook Time: 25 minutes

Total Time: 35 minutes

Servings: 4

Ingredients

- ➤ 4 tbsp. butter, divided
- ➤ ½ sleeve buttery round crackers (such as Ritz®), crushed
- ➤ 1 lb thick-cut cod loin
- ➤ ½ medium lemon, juiced
- ➤ ¼ cups of dry white wine
- ➤ 1 tbsp. diced fresh parsley
- ➤ 1 tbsp. diced green onion
- ➤ One medium lemon, cut into wedges

Directions

1. Amass all the ingredients.
2. Oven: 400 degrees Fahrenheit (200 degrees C).
3. An oven-safe bowl should contain 2 tbsp of butter. Melt in the microwave for 30 seconds on high. Round buttery crackers are mixed with melted butter.
4. In a 7x11-inch baking dish, add the final 2 tbsp of butter. In a preheated oven, melt for 1 to 3 minutes—dish out of the oven.
5. Put the cod in the baking dish and brush both sides with melted butter.
6. For 10 minutes, bake the cod in a preheated oven. Remove from oven and top with cracker and wine mixture. Return to the oven and bake for 10 minutes until the fish is opaque and flakes easily with a fork.
7. Lemon wedges should be served with the garnish of parsley and green onions.

76. Unbelievable Fish Batter

Prep Time: 10 minutes

Total Time: 10 minutes

Servings: 6

Ingredients

- ➤ 1 cup of all-purpose flour
- ➤ ½ cup of milk
- ➤ ½ cup of water
- ➤ ¼ cups of baking powder
- ➤ 1 tsp. salt

Directions

1. In a bowl, stir the flour, milk, water, baking powder, and salt until well combined.

77. Easy Tuna Patties

Prep Time: 15 minutes

Cook Time: 10 minutes

Total Time: 25 minutes

Servings: 4

Ingredients

- ➤ 2 eggs
- ➤ 2 tsp. lemon juice
- ➤ 10 tbsp. Italian-seasoned bread crumbs

- 3 tbsp. grated Parmesan cheese
- 3 (5 Oz.) cans tuna, drained
- 3 tbsp. diced onion
- One pinch of ground black pepper
- 3 tbsp. vegetable oil

Directions

1. Whisk together the eggs, lemon juice, and bread crumbs in a bowl. Add the Parmesan cheese and mix to form a paste. Black pepper should be added after thoroughly combining the tuna and onion.
2. Make eight 1-inch-thick patties out of the tuna mixture using your hands.
3. Over medium heat, a skillet is heated with vegetable oil. Patties should be fried in hot oil for five minutes on each side or until golden brown.

78. Southern Fried Catfish

Prep Time: 20 minutes

Cook Time: 10 minutes

Total Time: 30 minutes

Servings: 2

Ingredients

- ½ cup of buttermilk
- ½ cup of water
- salt and pepper, to taste

- ➢ 1 lb catfish fillets, cut into strips
- ➢ 1 ½ cups of fine cornmeal
- ➢ ½ cup of all-purpose flour
- ➢ 1 tsp. seafood seasoning, such as Old Bay™
- ➢ 1-quart vegetable oil for deep frying

Directions

1. Buttermilk, salt, and pepper must all be combined in a small bowl. Pour the mixture into a flat pan large enough to accommodate fillets. The pan should have the fillets in one layer, and they should be turned to coat all surfaces. To marinate, set aside

2. Mix cornmeal, flour, and seafood seasoning in a 2-gallon plastic bag that can be sealed. Add a few fillets and gently shake the bag to coat the fish with the coating.

3. To 365 degrees Fahrenheit, boil the oil in a deep fryer (185 degrees C).

4. In hot oil, fry fillets for about 3 minutes or until crisp and golden. Work in batches to avoid crowding, so the fillets have sufficient space to brown properly. Utilize paper towels to dry off.

79. Seared Ahi Tuna Steaks

Prep Time: 5 minutes

Cook Time: 2 minutes

Total Time: 7 minutes

Servings: 2

Ingredients

- ➤ 2 (5 Oz.) ahi tuna steaks
- ➤ 1 tsp. kosher salt
- ➤ ¼ tsp. cayenne pepper
- ➤ ½ tbsp. butter
- ➤ 2 tbsp. olive oil
- ➤ 1 tsp. whole peppercorns

Directions

1. Dry off tuna steaks and sprinkle salt and cayenne pepper on both sides of the fish.
2. Over medium-high heat, melt butter in a skillet.
3. Cook the peppercorns in the olive oil for about 5 minutes or until they soften and pop.
4. Cook the tuna in the skillet gently for up to 1 1/2 minutes per side or until it reaches the desired degree of doneness.
5. To serve, cut tuna into slices that are 1/4 inch thick.

80. Simple Broiled Haddock

Prep Time: 10 minutes

Cook Time: 10 minutes

Total Time: 20 minutes

Servings: 4

Ingredients

- ➤ 2 lbs haddock fillets
- ➤ ½ tsp. onion powder
- ➤ ½ tsp. paprika
- ➤ ½ tsp. garlic powder
- ➤ ½ tsp. ground black pepper
- ➤ ½ tsp. Salt
- ➤ ¼ tsp. cayenne pepper
- ➤ 1 tbsp. butter, cut into small pieces
- ➤ One lemon, cut into wedges

Directions

1. Preheat the broiler while positioning an oven rack about 6 inches from the heat source. Spray cooking spray on a baking sheet after lining it with aluminum foil.
2. On the prepared baking sheet, arrange the haddock fillets.
3. Combine the cayenne pepper, salt, black pepper, onion powder, and paprika in a small bowl. Sprinkle the mixture over the fish, then top with butter.
4. For 6 to 8 minutes, or until the fish flakes easily with a fork, broil the food in a preheated oven. Lemon wedges are optional.

81.   Homemade Pasta Roni

Prep Time: 5 minutes

Cook Time: 10 minutes

Total Time: 15 minutes

Servings: 2

Ingredients

- ➢ 2 cups of chicken broth
- ➢ 3 Oz. angel hair pasta
- ➢ 1 tbsp. butter
- ➢ One clove of garlic, minced
- ➢ ½ tsp. Italian seasoning
- ➢ ¼ cups of heavy cream
- ➢ ¾ cups of finely shredded Parmesan cheese
- ➢ 1 tsp. minced fresh parsley, or to taste

Directions

1. Over medium-high heat, bring a pot of chicken broth to a boil. Angel hair pasta should be cooked in the boiling broth for 4 to 5 minutes, stirring occasionally, until tender but firm to the bite.
2. Drain the pasta and set aside 1/4 cup of the chicken broth.
3. In a saucepan, melt the butter over low heat. Stir in the garlic, and cook for 30 seconds or until fragrant. Add the whipping cream, Italian seasoning, and 1/4 cup of the

chicken broth set aside. Melt the Parmesan cheese after adding it.

4. Add the angel hair pasta and mix well. Freshly minced parsley is used as a garnish.

82.   Quick and Easy Pancit

Prep Time: 15 minutes

Cook Time: 15 minutes

Total Time: 30 minutes

Servings: 6

Ingredients

- ➢ 1 (12 Oz.) package of dried rice noodles
- ➢ 1 tsp. vegetable oil
- ➢ One onion, finely diced
- ➢ Three cloves garlic, minced
- ➢ 2 cups of diced cooked chicken breast meat
- ➢ One small head of cabbage, thinly sliced
- ➢ Four carrots, thinly sliced
- ➢ ¼ cups of soy sauce
- ➢ Two lemons - cut into wedges for garnish

Directions

1. Rice noodles should be placed in a sizable bowl, covered with warm water, and softened for 8 to 10 minutes. Drain and reserve.

2. Oil should be heated in a large skillet or wok simultaneously. Add the onion and garlic; stir-fry for 3 to 5 minutes or until the onion is soft. Add the soy sauce, chicken, cabbage, and carrots. Until the cabbage starts to soften, cook. Add the noodles and stir continuously until heated all the way through.
3. After transferring the pancit to a serving dish, add lemon wedges as a garnish.

83. To Die For Fettuccine Alfredo

Prep Time: 15 minutes

Cook Time: 15 minutes

Total Time: 30 minutes

Servings: 6

Ingredients

- ➤ 24 Oz. dry fettuccine pasta
- ➤ 1 cup of butter
- ➤ ¾ pint heavy cream
- ➤ salt and pepper to taste
- ➤ One dash of garlic salt
- ➤ ¾ cups of grated Romano cheese
- ➤ ½ cup of grated Parmesan cheese

Directions

1. Bring to a boil a sizable pot of lightly salted water. After adding the fettuccine, cook it for 8 to 10 minutes, or until it's al dente, then drain.
2. Salt, pepper, and garlic salt are added to the melted butter and cream in a big saucepan over low heat. The heat should be medium; stir in the grated Romano and Parmesan cheese once the sauce has thickened.
3. Serve the sauce-coated pasta immediately after adding the cooked pasta and thoroughly mixing.

84. Pesto Pasta

Prep Time: 5 minutes

Cook Time: 10 minutes

Total Time: 15 minutes

Servings: 8

Ingredients

- ➢ 1 (16 Oz.) package of pasta
- ➢ 2 tbsp. olive oil
- ➢ ½ cup of diced onion
- ➢ 2 ½ tbsp. pesto
- ➢ salt to taste
- ➢ ground black pepper to taste
- ➢ 2 tbsp. grated Parmesan cheese

Directions

1. Bring water to a big pot lightly salted to a rolling boil. Regain the boil after adding the pasta. Pasta should be cooked uncovered for 8 to 10 minutes, stirring once or twice, until tender but firm to the bite. Drain and then place in a big bowl.
2. Over medium-low heat, warm oil in a frying pan. Add onion; stir-fry and cook for 3 minutes or until soft. Once heated through, stir in pesto, salt, and pepper.
3. Add the pesto mixture to the hot pasta, add the grated cheese, and toss to combine.

85. Pan-Seared Tilapia

Prep Time: 5 minutes

Cook Time: 10 minutes

Total Time: 15 minutes

Servings: 4

Ingredients

- ➢ 4 (4 Oz.) tilapia fillets
- ➢ salt and ground black pepper to taste
- ➢ ½ cup of all-purpose flour
- ➢ 1 tbsp. olive oil
- ➢ 2 tbsp. unsalted butter, melted
- ➢ 1 tbsp. lemon juice, or to taste
- ➢ 1 tsp. diced fresh flat-leaf parsley, or to taste

> ½ tsp. diced fresh thyme, or to taste

Directions

1. Use paper towels to dry off the tilapia fillets after giving them a cold water rinse. Each fillet should be salted and peppered on both sides.
2. Fill a shallow dish with flour. To coat each fillet, gently press it into the flour and shake off any extra.
3. A big skillet with medium-high heat is used to heat the olive oil. If necessary, cook the tilapia fillets in batches in the hot oil until the fish flakes easily when tested with a fork, about 4 minutes per side.
4. The final moment before removing the tilapia fillets from the skillet, brush melted butter on top of them.
5. Lemon juice should drizzle over the fillets before parsley and thyme are added as a garnish.

86. Easy Garlic-Lemon Scallops

Prep Time: 10 minutes

Cook Time: 5 minutes

Total Time: 15 minutes

Servings: 6

Ingredients

> ¾ cups of butter
> 3 tbsp. minced garlic
> 2 lbs large sea scallops

- ➤ 2 tbsp. fresh lemon juice
- ➤ 1 tsp. salt
- ➤ ⅛ tsp. pepper

Directions

1. Over medium heat, melt butter in a sizable skillet. Add the garlic and stir for a couple of seconds until fragrant.
2. Place the scallops in the skillet in a single layer and cook for 2 minutes or until one side is golden brown. Use tongs to flip the scallops over, then cook for another 2 minutes or until opaque and firm. While reserving the butter in the skillet, transfer the scallops to a platter.
3. Scallops are served with a butter sauce flavored with lemon juice, salt, and pepper.

87.   Black Beans and Rice

Prep Time: 5 minutes

Cook Time: 25 minutes

Total Time: 30 minutes

Servings: 6

Ingredients

- ➤ 1 tsp. olive oil
- ➤ One onion, diced
- ➤ Two cloves garlic, minced
- ➤ ¾ cups of uncooked white rice
- ➤ 1 ½ cups of low sodium, low-fat vegetable broth

- ➤ 3 ½ cups of canned black beans, drained
- ➤ 1 tsp. ground cumin
- ➤ ¼ tsp. cayenne pepper

Directions

1. Over medium-high heat, warm oil in a pan. Cook and stir the onion and garlic for about 4 minutes or until the onion has softened. After coating the rice, add it, cook, and stir it for 2 minutes.
2. When it starts to boil, add the vegetable broth. Cook with the lid on for about 20 minutes, reducing the heat to a simmer.
3. Stir in the beans, cumin, and cayenne; heat through the beans.

88. Buttered Noodles

Prep Time: 5 minutes

Cook Time: 15 minutes

Total Time: 20 minutes

Servings: 8

Ingredients

- ➤ 1 (16 Oz.) package of fettuccine noodles
- ➤ 6 tbsp. butter, cut into pieces
- ➤ ⅓ cups of grated Parmesan cheese
- ➤ salt and ground black pepper to taste

Directions

1. Amass all the ingredients.
2. Bring water to a big pot lightly salted to a rolling boil.
3. Add the fettuccine, bring the mixture back to a boil, and cook the pasta for 8 to 10 minutes on a medium heat setting or until it is firm to the bite.
4. Put the pasta back in the pot after draining. Pasta should be evenly coated with butter, Parmesan cheese, salt, and pepper.

89.   Simple Broiled Haddock

Prep Time: 10 minutes

Cook Time: 10 minutes

Total Time: 20 minutes

Servings: 4

Ingredients

- ➢ 2 lbs haddock fillets
- ➢ ½ tsp. onion powder
- ➢ ½ tsp. paprika
- ➢ ½ tsp. garlic powder
- ➢ ½ tsp. ground black pepper
- ➢ ½ tsp. Salt
- ➢ ¼ tsp. cayenne pepper
- ➢ 1 tbsp. butter, cut into small pieces
- ➢ One lemon, cut into wedges

Directions

1. Preheat the broiler while positioning an oven rack about 6 inches from the heat source. Spray cooking spray on an aluminum foil-lined baking sheet.
2. On the prepared baking sheet, arrange the haddock fillets.
3. Combine the cayenne pepper, salt, black pepper, onion powder, and paprika in a small bowl. Sprinkle the mixture over the fish, then top with butter.
4. For 6 to 8 minutes, or until the fish flakes easily with a fork, broil the food in a preheated oven. Lemon wedges are optional.

90. Easy Lasagna

Prep Time: 10 minutes

Cook Time: 1 hour 10 minutes

Additional Time: 10 minutes

Total Time: 1 hour 30 minutes

Servings: 12

Ingredients

- ➢ 1 lb lean ground beef
- ➢ 1 (32 Oz.) jar spaghetti sauce
- ➢ 32 Oz. cottage cheese
- ➢ 3 cups of shredded mozzarella cheese, divided
- ➢ Two eggs
- ➢ ½ cup of grated Parmesan cheese

- ➤ 2 tsp. dried parsley
- ➤ salt to taste
- ➤ ground black pepper to taste
- ➤ Nine lasagna noodles
- ➤ ½ cup of water

Directions

1. Oven: 350 degrees Fahrenheit (175 degrees C).
2. Over medium-high heat, preheat a sizable skillet. For 8 to 10 minutes, brown and crumble the ground beef in a hot skillet while stirring frequently. Dispose of grease by draining it. Add spaghetti sauce, then simmer for five minutes.
3. Mix the cottage cheese, 2 cups of mozzarella cheese, eggs, 1/2 cup of grated Parmesan cheese, dried parsley, salt, and pepper in a sizable bowl.
4. A 9x13-inch baking dish should be covered in 3/4 cup of sauce. Three uncooked lasagna noodles, 1 3/4 cups of the cheese mixture, and 1/4 cups of sauce should be placed on top; repeat layers two more times. Add the final three noodles, sauce, mozzarella, and Parmesan cheese. Along the dish's edges, pour 1/2 cup of water. Aluminum foil should be tightly wrapped.
5. Bake for 45 minutes in the preheated oven. Bake for ten more minutes after removing the cover. Before serving, let stand for ten minutes.

91. Fish in Foil

Prep Time: 10 minutes

Cook Time: 15 minutes

Total Time: 25 minutes

Servings: 2

Ingredients

- ➤ Two rainbow trout fillets
- ➤ 1 tbsp. olive oil
- ➤ 2 tsp. garlic salt
- ➤ 1 tsp. ground black pepper
- ➤ Two sheets of heavy-duty aluminum foil
- ➤ One fresh jalapeno pepper, sliced
- ➤ One lemon, sliced

Directions

1. Oven: 400 degrees Fahrenheit (200 degrees C).
2. After rinsing, pat the fillets dry. Garlic salt and black pepper are sprinkled on the olive oil-rubbed fillets. Each fillet should be put on a sizable piece of aluminum foil. Jalapeno slices should be placed on top, and the fillets should be drenched in lemon juice from the ends. Top the fillets with the remaining lemon slices.
3. To create packets that are enclosed, carefully seal the foil's edges. Packets should be put on a baking sheet.
4. Depending on the size of the fillets, bake for 15 to 20 minutes in the preheated oven or until the fish flakes easily with a fork.

92.   Pesto Pasta with Chicken

Prep Time: 10 minutes

Cook Time: 20 minutes

Total Time: 30 minutes

Servings: 8

Ingredients

- 1 (16 Oz.) package bow tie pasta
- 1 tsp. olive oil
- Two cloves garlic, minced
- Two skinless, boneless chicken breasts cut into bite-sized pieces
- 1 pinch crushed red pepper flakes, or to taste
- ½ cup of pesto sauce
- ⅓ cups of oil-packed sun-dried tomatoes, drained and cut into strips

Directions

1. Bring to a boil a sizable pot of lightly salted water. For 8 to 10 minutes, add the pasta and cook until al dente; drain.
2. Over medium heat, warm oil in a big skillet. After cooking the garlic, stir in the chicken and red pepper flakes until it's soft. Cook chicken until golden and fully cooked.
3. Mix the pasta, chicken, sun-dried tomatoes, and pesto in a sizable bowl. Toss to coat evenly.

93. Linguine with Clam Sauce

Prep Time: 5 minutes

Cook Time: 15 minutes

Total Time: 20 minutes

Servings: 4

Ingredients

- 1 (16 Oz.) package of linguini pasta
- 2 (6.5 Oz.) cans of minced clams with juice
- ½ cup of vegetable oil
- ¼ cups of butter
- 1 tbsp. dried parsley
- ¼ tbsp. dried basil
- ½ tsp. minced garlic
- ground black pepper to taste

Directions

1. Bring to a boil a sizable pot of lightly salted water. Cook the linguine for about 11 minutes at a boil until it is soft to the bite but still firm. Drain.
2. Clams, juice, oil, butter, parsley, basil, garlic, and pepper, should be combined in a sizable saucepan while the pasta cooks. Until boiling, cook over medium heat.
3. Over warm pasta, spoon warm clam sauce.

94.   Sweet and Sour Meatballs

Prep Time: 5 minutes

Cook Time: 15 minutes

Total Time: 20 minutes

Servings: 5

Ingredients
Meatballs:

- 1 lb ground beef
- 1 cup of dry bread crumbs
- One onion, diced
- One egg
- salt and pepper to taste

Sweet and Sour Sauce:

- 1 cup of brown sugar
- 1 cup of water
- ½ cup of ketchup
- ½ cup of cider vinegar
- 2 tbsp. soy sauce
- 2 tbsp. cornstarch

Directions

1. Making meatballs requires thoroughly mixing beef, bread crumbs, onion, egg, salt, and pepper in a large bowl.
2. Roll the mixture into balls with one 1/2-inch diameter.
3. Cook the meatballs in a sizable nonstick skillet over medium heat until thoroughly cooked.

4. Making sauce In a medium bowl, whisk together the brown sugar, water, ketchup, vinegar, soy sauce, and cornstarch until smooth.
5. Add sauce to meatballs. Simmer for 3 to 5 minutes with low heat until the sauce is thick.

95. Sirloin Steak with Garlic Butter

Prep Time: 20 minutes

Cook Time: 10 minutes

Total Time: 30 minutes

Servings: 8

Ingredients

- ½ cup of butter
- Four cloves garlic, minced
- 2 tsp. garlic powder
- 4 lbs beef top sirloin steaks
- salt and pepper to taste

Directions

1. High heat should be set on an outdoor grill before lightly oiling the grates.
2. Melt the butter in a small saucepan over low heat; add the minced garlic and garlic powder, and stir. Set apart.
3. Each steak should have salt and pepper on both sides.
4. Steaks should be cooked on a preheated grill for 4 to 5 minutes on each side. An instant-read thermometer inserted

in the center should register 140 degrees Fahrenheit (60 degrees Celsius) for medium doneness.

5. Transfer steaks to warmed plates, liberally brush tops with garlic butter and let rest for 2 to 3 minutes before serving.

96. Chicago-Style Hot Dog

Prep Time: 10 minutes

Cook Time: 5 minutes

Total Time: 15 minutes

Servings: 1

Ingredients

- One all-beef hot dog
- One poppy seed hot dog bun
- 1 tbsp. yellow mustard
- 1 tbsp. sweet green pickle relish
- 1 tbsp. diced onion
- Four tomato wedges
- One dill pickle spear
- Two sport peppers
- One dash of celery salt

Directions

1. High heat is used to bring a pot of water to a boil. Turn the heat down to low, add the hot dog to the water, and heat it for about five minutes. The hot dog should be taken out of the water and put aside.

2. Steam the poppy seed bun for about two minutes in a steamer basket in the pot.
3. Steamed bun with a hot dog inside. Put the following toppings on top: celery salt, mustard, relish, onion, tomato, and pickles. On one side, sandwich the tomato wedges between the top of the bun and the hot dog. On the other side, place a pickle between the bottom of the bun and the hot dog. Ketchup should not even be considered!

97. Baked Fresh Rainbow Trout

Prep Time: 10 minutes

Cook Time: 20 minutes

Total Time: 30 minutes

Servings: 6

Ingredients
- 2 tsp. olive oil, divided
- Two whole rainbow trout gutted and cleaned, heads and tails still on
- ¼ tsp. dried dill weed
- ¼ tsp. dried thyme
- salt to taste
- ½ large onion, sliced
- Two thin slices of lemon
- 2 tbsp. hot water
- ground black pepper to taste

Directions

1. Oven: 400 degrees Fahrenheit (200 degrees C). 1 tsp. Olive oil should be used to grease a 9x13-inch baking dish.
2. With the remaining olive oil, coat the trout in the baking dish that has been prepared. Assemble the components for the seasoning.
3. Dill, thyme, and salt are used to season the inside and outside of the fish. Sprinkle pepper on top after stuffing each fish with onion slices. Put a slice of lemon on each fish.
4. Add hot water to the dish after 10 minutes of baking in the preheated oven. Ten more minutes of baking is required until the fish flakes easily with a fork.

98. Crab Legs with Garlic Butter Sauce

Prep Time: 5 minutes

Cook Time: 15 minutes

Total Time: 20 minutes

Servings: 2

Ingredients

- ➤ 1 lb Snow Crab clusters, thawed if necessary
- ➤ ¼ cups of butter
- ➤ One clove of garlic, minced
- ➤ 1 ½ tsp. dried parsley
- ➤ ¼ tsp. freshly ground black pepper
- ➤ ⅛ tsp. salt

Directions

1. Each crab piece should have a lengthwise slit made in its shell.
2. Over medium heat, melt butter in a sizable skillet. Cook the garlic for 1 to 2 minutes until it becomes translucent. Add salt, pepper, and parsley by stirring. Heat the mixture further until it bubbles.
3. Add the crab legs and stir to coat with the butter mixture. Simmer for 5–6 minutes or until everything is thoroughly heated.

99. Baby Spinach Omelet

Prep Time: 5 minutes

Cook Time: 10 minutes

Total Time: 15 minutes

Servings: 1

Ingredients

➢ Two eggs
➢ 1 cup of torn baby spinach leaves
➢ 1 ½ tbsp. grated Parmesan cheese
➢ ¼ tsp. onion powder
➢ ⅛ tsp. ground nutmeg
➢ salt and pepper to taste

Directions

1. In a bowl, whisk the eggs. Next, add the baby spinach and Parmesan cheese. Add salt, pepper, nutmeg, and onion powder for seasoning.
2. Apply cooking spray to a small skillet and heat it over medium heat. Add the egg mixture once it's warm, and cook for 3 minutes or until it's partially set. After flipping with a spatula, cook for another two to three minutes.
3. When the omelet is the desired doneness, reduce heat to low and cook for another 2 to 3 minutes.

100. Best Ever Crab Cakes

Prep Time: 15 minutes

Cook Time: 10 minutes

Total Time: 25 minutes

Servings: 4

Ingredients

- One egg
- 3 tbsp. mayonnaise
- 1 tbsp. minced green onions
- Four tsp. lemon juice
- 1 tsp. dried tarragon
- ⅛ tsp. red pepper flakes
- 8 Oz. crabmeat
- ½ cup of crushed buttery round crackers

> 1 tbsp. butter

Directions

1. Egg, mayonnaise, green onions, lemon juice, tarragon, and pepper flakes are mixed in a medium bowl. Add the crabmeat gently, being careful not to break up the meat. Add cracker crumbs gradually while blending until the desired consistency is reached. Make four patties out of the crab mixture.
2. In a skillet over medium heat, melt the butter.
3. Patties should be cooked in a skillet for 5 to 6 minutes on each side or until golden brown.

Chapter 6: Poultry, Beef, and Pork Recipes

101. Cornish Hens the Easy Way

Prep Time: 5 minutes

Cook Time: 45 minutes

Additional Time: 10 minutes

Total Time: 1 hour

Servings: 4

Ingredients

- ➤ 4 Cornish game hens
- ➤ Two limes halved
- ➤ 2 tsp. olive oil
- ➤ ¼ tsp. chili powder
- ➤ ¼ tsp. ground cumin
- ➤ To taste, add kosher salt and black pepper.

Directions

1. Oven: 425 degrees Fahrenheit (220 degrees C).
2. Use a lime half to rub the chickens. Olive oil should be drizzled over the dish before being seasoned with cumin, kosher salt, and black pepper. In a shallow roasting pan, arrange the hens on a rack.
3. Hens are roasted for 15 minutes in a preheated oven.
4. Lower the oven's setting to 350 degrees Fahrenheit (175 degrees C).
5. After 30 minutes, the meat should no longer be pink at the bone, and the juices should run clear. The thickest part of the thigh, close to the bone, should register 165 degrees Fahrenheit on an instant-read thermometer (74 degrees C). After removing from the oven, cover with two sheets of aluminum foil and let the food rest for 10 minutes before cutting.

102. Baked Cornish Game Hens

Prep Time: 30 minutes

Cook Time: 1 hour 30 minutes

Total Time: 2 hours

Servings: 4

Ingredients

- ➢ 2 Cornish game hens
- ➢ ½ cup of melted butter
- ➢ ½ onion, diced
- ➢ ½ stalk celery, diced
- ➢ ¼ green bell pepper, diced
- ➢ 1 (4.5 Oz.) can mushrooms, drained and diced
- ➢ Two cloves garlic, minced
- ➢ 1 tbsp. dried basil
- ➢ 1 tsp. dried oregano
- ➢ 1 tbsp. diced fresh parsley
- ➢ ¼ cups of melted butter

Directions

1. Three hundred twenty-five degrees Fahrenheit in the oven (165 degrees C).
2. Mix the onion, celery, bell pepper, mushrooms, garlic, basil, oregano, and parsley with 1/2 cup of melted butter in a small bowl.
3. Put equal parts of the butter/vegetable mixture inside each hen after seasoning them inside and out with salt and pepper to taste. Stuff the birds, breast side up, in a 9 x 13-inch baking dish. 14 cups of melted butter should be drizzled on.

4. Bake the dish with a cover for 1 1/2 hours in a preheated oven. At 500 degrees F, remove the cover and brown (260 degrees C).

103. Orange Glazed Cornish Hen

Prep Time: 15 minutes

Cook Time: 1 hour

Additional Time: 1 hour

Total Time: 2 hours 15 minutes

Servings: 2

Ingredients
Marinade:

- 2 tbsp. olive oil
- 1 tbsp. Dijon mustard
- One lemon, zested and juiced
- One orange, zested and juiced
- Three cloves garlic, diced
- 1 tsp. kosher salt
- freshly ground black pepper to taste
- Two Cornish game hens

Sauce:

- Two cups of orange juice
- ½ cup of soy sauce
- ½ cup of honey

- ➢ ¼ cups of Dijon mustard
- ➢ ¼ cups of finely diced onion
- ➢ 2 tsp. ground ginger
- ➢ black pepper freshly ground to taste

Directions

1. Olive oil, 1 tbsp. Dijon mustard, orange, lemon juices, garlic, salt, and black pepper are all combined in a sizable resealable bag. Hens should be added, the bag should be closed, and the marinade should be applied to the hens. Put the bag in the refrigerator for an hour, flipping it once or twice to redistribute the marinade.
2. Four hundred fifty degrees Fahrenheit should be set for the oven (230 degrees C).
3. Combine orange juice, soy sauce, honey, ginger, onion, 1/4 cup of Dijon mustard, and black pepper in a bowl.
4. After removing the hens from the marinade, transfer them to a roasting pan and discard the marinade.
5. In the preheated oven, roast the hens for 50 minutes. After five more minutes of roasting, glaze the hens with orange. Turn the hens over, brush with additional glaze, and roast for 5 minutes or until the meat is no longer pink in the center. A nearby bone-injured instant-read thermometer should register 165 degrees Fahrenheit (74 degrees C).

104. Seasoned Cornish Hens

Prep Time: 15 minutes

Cook Time: 1 hour

Additional Time: 15 minutes

Total Time: 1 hour 30 minutes

Servings: 4

Ingredients

- ½ cup of soy sauce
- 2 tbsp. oyster sauce
- Three cloves garlic, peeled and crushed
- ground black pepper to taste
- Two large Cornish game hens
- 2 tbsp. butter

Directions

1. Oven: 325 degrees Fahrenheit (165 degrees C).
2. Soy sauce, oyster sauce, garlic, and pepper should all be combined in a big bowl. Cornish game hens should marinate in the mixture for 10 minutes.
3. Add the marinade mixture to the hens' medium baking dish before placing it in the oven. Bake the dish for 30 minutes in a preheated oven with the foil covering.
4. Place 1 tbsp. Of butter on each hen after removing the dish's cover. To 350 degrees Fahrenheit in the oven (175 degrees C). Bake the hens for another 30 minutes, often basting with the marinade mixture, or until the outside is crisp and lightly browned, the inside is no longer pink, and the juices are clear.

105. Best Chicken Patties

Prep Time: 25 minutes

Cook Time: 10 minutes

Total Time: 35 minutes

Servings: 6

Ingredients

- 18 Oz. ground chicken
- One onion, finely diced
- One bunch of fresh parsley, finely diced
- One large egg
- Two cloves garlic, crushed, or more to taste
- sea salt and freshly ground black pepper to taste
- Two tbsp. mayonnaise
- ¼ cups of all-purpose flour, or as needed
- 3 tbsp. vegetable oil

Directions

1. Chicken, onion, parsley, egg, garlic, sea salt, and pepper should all be combined in a bowl. The mixture will be very soft after you add the mayonnaise and stir to combine.
2. In a small bowl, add the flour. Large spoonfuls of the chicken mixture should be dropped into the flour. Roll to coat, then gently press into patties.
3. Over medium-high heat, preheat the oil in a skillet. 5 to 7 minutes per side, cook the chicken patties in the hot oil until golden brown and no longer pink in the center.

106. Quinoa Chicken

Prep Time: 10 minutes

Cook Time: 30 minutes

Total Time: 40 minutes

Servings: 6

Ingredients

- ➢ 2 cups of chicken broth
- ➢ 1 cup of quinoa
- ➢ 2 tsp. vegetable oil, or as needed
- ➢ ½ onion, diced
- ➢ Two cloves garlic, or to taste, minced
- ➢ 1 ½ lbs ground chicken
- ➢ 1 ½ (10 Oz.) cans diced tomatoes with green chile peppers

Directions

1. In a saucepan, bring quinoa and chicken broth to a boil. When the quinoa is tender and the water has been absorbed, reduce the heat to medium-low, cover the pot, and simmer for 15 to 20 minutes.
2. In the meantime, warm up the oil in a sizable skillet over medium-high heat. In hot oil, sauté onion, and garlic for about 5 minutes, or until onion turns translucent. Cook and stir the ground chicken for 5 to 7 minutes, until it is browned and crumbly.
3. Add diced tomatoes and cooked quinoa to the chicken mixture; simmer for an additional 10 minutes to allow flavors to meld.

107. Keto Chicken Crust Pizza

Prep Time: 10 minutes

Cook Time: 35 minutes

Total Time: 45 minutes

Servings: 4

Ingredients

- 1 lb ground chicken
- ½ cup of mozzarella cheese, shredded
- ¼ cups of freshly grated Parmesan cheese
- Three cloves garlic, minced
- 1 tsp. Italian seasoning
- ½ tsp. salt
- ¼ tsp. pepper
- 1 tbsp. diced fresh basil

Directions

1. Oven: 400 degrees Fahrenheit (200 degrees C). Put parchment paper on a baking sheet to line it.
2. Use your hands to thoroughly combine the mozzarella, Parmesan, garlic, Italian seasoning, salt, and pepper in the large bowl with the ground chicken. Basil is added after folding.
3. The chicken mixture should be sandwiched between two sheets of parchment paper. Spread the mixture into a circle or rectangle with a 1/4- to 1/2-inch thickness by gently

pressing on the top piece of parchment. The top parchment piece should be taken off and discarded.

4. Bake in a preheated oven for 35 to 45 minutes or until the edges brown.

108. Thai Chicken Larb

Prep Time: 20 minutes

Cook Time: 10 minutes

Total Time: 30 minutes

Servings: 4

Ingredients

- 1 lb ground chicken
- One red onion halved and thinly sliced
- ¼ cups of sliced scallions
- One lime, juiced
- 2 tbsp. diced fresh cilantro
- 1 tbsp. finely diced fresh mint
- 2 tsp. minced fresh ginger
- 1 tsp. lemongrass paste
- 1 tsp. fish sauce, or more to taste
- 1 tsp. red pepper flakes, or more to taste
- 1 tsp. sea salt

Directions

1. Over medium heat, preheat a sizable skillet. Insert chicken. Cook and stir the chicken for about 5 minutes or until it is

broken into small pieces. Include scallions and red onions. The chicken should be cooked for another 2 minutes, breaking it up as it cooks. Add fish sauce, red pepper flakes, ginger, mint, cilantro, and lemongrass. For another three minutes, continue to cook and stir while doing so. Use sea salt as a seasoning.

109. Chicken Meatballs

Prep Time: 20 minutes

Cook Time: 20 minutes

Additional Time: 15 minutes

Total Time: 55 minutes

Servings: 6

Ingredients

> 1 lb ground chicken
> One egg, beaten
> ¼ cups of low-fat cream cheese
> ¼ cups of grated Parmesan cheese
> Four cloves garlic, grated
> 1 ½ tbsp. olive oil
> 1 tbsp. dry bread crumbs
> 2 tsp. diced fresh basil
> 1 tsp. crushed red pepper
> 1 tsp. garlic powder
> ½ tsp. sea salt

- ½ tsp. black pepper
- ½ tsp. dried parsley
- ½ tsp. dried oregano
- 1 cup of diced fresh mozzarella or as needed

Directions

1. Oven: 425 degrees Fahrenheit (220 degrees C).
2. In a bowl that can be put in the freezer, mix the ingredients: ground chicken, egg, cream cheese, Parmesan cheese, garlic, olive oil, bread crumbs, basil, red pepper, garlic powder, salt, pepper, parsley, and oregano. The mixture will become firmer and easier to handle after 15 minutes in the freezer.
3. Utilizing an ice cream scoop, shape into 14 meatballs of equal size. Make sure the mozzarella cheese is completely encased by meat before placing a piece in the center of each meatball. On a nonstick baking sheet, arrange the meatballs.
4. Bake for 20 to 25 minutes or until the juices are clear and the centers are no longer pink.

110. Air Fryer Chicken Kyiv Balls

Prep Time: 15 minutes

Cook Time: 10 minutes

Additional Time: 30 minutes

Total Time: 55 minutes

Servings: 12

Ingredients

- ½ cup of unsalted butter softened
- 2 tbsp. diced fresh flat-leaf parsley
- Two cloves garlic, crushed
- 1 (19.1 Oz.) package of ground chicken breast
- 2 eggs, beaten
- 1 cup of panko bread crumbs
- 1 tsp. paprika
- 1 tsp. salt
- ½ tsp. ground black pepper
- cooking spray

Directions

1. In a bowl, combine butter, parsley, and garlic and stir to combine. Place the mixture on a baking sheet in 12 equal portions. About 20 minutes of freezing time is required.
2. Make 12 balls out of ground chicken. In the center of each ball, make a deep thumbprint. In the depression, place a piece of herbed butter frozen, then completely encase the butter in the meat. The remaining balls, and repeat.
3. A bowl should contain beaten eggs. Combine the panko, paprika, salt, and pepper in another bowl.
4. One ground chicken ball should be dipped in the beaten eggs first, followed by the seasoned bread crumbs. The ball should be re-dipped in the egg and the seasoned bread crumbs. The remaining balls, and repeat. Freeze for 10 minutes after placing on a baking sheet.
5. Set an air fryer to 400 degrees Fahrenheit (200 degrees C). Spray half of the balls with nonstick cooking spray before placing them in the air fryer.

6. 5 minutes of cooking. Use tongs to flip the balls over, then re-spray them with nonstick cooking oil. Cook for a further five minutes. The remaining chicken balls, and repeat.

111. Sous Vide Beef Tenderloin Roast

Cook Time: 2 hours 40 minutes

Chill Time: 8 hours

Rest Time: 10 minutes

Total Time: 10 hours 50 minutes

Servings: 10

Ingredients

- 4 ½ lbs whole beef tenderloin
- 1 tbsp. sea salt/kosher salt
- 1 tsp. freshly ground black pepper or more to taste
- 6 cloves garlic
- 3 fresh thyme sprigs, or to taste
- rosemary sprig
- 3 tbsp. unsalted butter, divided or more as needed
- 2 tbsp. olive oil, or as needed
- 1 splash of red wine
- 1 tbsp. gelatin powder
- 1 cup of cold water
- salt and freshly ground black pepper to taste

Directions

1. The day before cooking, trim the tenderloin and tie it together with kitchen twine. Mix the tenderloin with salt and pepper after combining them in a bowl. Place on a baking rack over a cookie sheet and let stand overnight, uncovered, in the fridge.

2. Tenderloin, garlic, thyme, and rosemary should be placed in sous vide vacuum bag the night before, and the bag should be sealed with a vacuum sealer. Save in the fridge until you're ready to sous vide.

3. Put a sou vide cooker on top of a heat-resistant water container and set the temperature to 133 degrees F. (56 degrees C). Depending on thickness, sous vide the tenderloin for 2 1/2 to 3 hours until it reaches the desired temperature.

4. Sprinkle gelatin powder on top of the water in a metal bowl and sit for about 30 minutes. Wait 30 minutes to see if the gelatin blooms. Stirring until a clear liquid form, place on top of a double boiler over simmering water. Don't allow water to boil.

5. Pull the tenderloin from the sous vide, pat it dry, and set it aside to rest while you make the gravy.

6. Pour the au jus liquids into the sous vide bag in a saucepan. Add one to two tbsp of butter and some red wine. Depending on the desired thickness, add as much of the bloomed gelatin and whisk until thoroughly combined. To taste, add herbs, pepper, and salt to the gravy.

7. A medium-high heat should be used for a cast iron pan. Olive oil should be brushed on the tenderloin before searing it for 1 to 2 minutes per side in a hot pan until it is well-browned.

If needed, melt extra butter in the pan. Tent with foil after removing from pan and let sit for five to ten minutes.

8. With gravy, slice the tenderloin.

112. Beef Ragu

Prep Time: 20 minutes

Cook Time: 3 hours

Total Time: 3 hours 20 minutes

Servings: 4

Ingredients

- ➢ 2 tbsp. olive oil
- ➢ 1 (2 lb) boneless beef chuck roast, cut into 2-inch cubes
- ➢ 1 tsp. ground black pepper
- ➢ 3 tsp. kosher salt, divided
- ➢ 1 yellow onion, diced
- ➢ 6 cloves garlic, diced
- ➢ 2 tbsp. harissa
- ➢ 2 tbsp. tomato paste
- ➢ 1 cup of dry red wine
- ➢ 1 (28 Oz.) can of crushed tomatoes
- ➢ One bay leaf
- ➢ 1 lb pappardelle pasta, cooked and drained
- ➢ grated Parmesan cheese, for serving

Directions

1. Over medium-high heat, preheat the oil in a big Dutch oven. Chuck roast should be peppered and salted with two tsp... Working in batches if necessary, brown the meat for about 10 minutes on all sides. Transfer to a big plate after removing from the Dutch oven.

2. Stir in onion as the heat is reduced to medium. Cook for about 8 minutes, frequently stirring until softened. Add the garlic and stir continuously for about a minute until fragrant. Add the harissa and tomato paste, and cook and stir for 2 minutes or until the mixture turns golden.

3. Pour in the wine and simmer for about 5 minutes, or until it has reduced by two-thirds, scraping up any browned bits on the bottom of the pot as you go. Add the bay leaf, chuck roast, tomatoes, and lastly 1 tsp of salt. Reduce the heat to medium while covering the pan. Cook the meat for approximately two and a half hours, stirring occasionally, or until it is fork-tender, the sauce has thickened, and the flavors have melded.

4. Eliminate and discard the bay leaf. To shred the meat, remove it from the Dutch oven and place it on a cutting board. Add pappardelle and the meat back to the pot. Grated Parmesan cheese is added on top.

113. Ground Beef Stroganoff Noodles

Prep Time: 10 minutes

Cook Time: 30 minutes

Total Time: 40 minutes

Servings: 4

Ingredients

- ➢ 1 tbsp. unsalted butter
- ➢ 1 tbsp. vegetable oil
- ➢ 1 cup of thinly sliced mushrooms
- ➢ 1 tsp. salt, plus more to taste
- ➢ ½ cup of diced onion
- ➢ 1 lb ground beef
- ➢ freshly ground black pepper
- ➢ One pinch of cayenne pepper
- ➢ Two cloves of minced garlic
- ➢ One ⅓ tbsp. flour
- ➢ 2 tbsp. vodka
- ➢ 2 ½ cups of beef broth, or as needed
- ➢ 1 cup of water
- ➢ 2 ½ cups of egg noodles
- ➢ ½ cup of sour cream, plus more for serving
- ➢ 2 tbsp. fresh sliced chives or green onions

Directions

1. Butter and oil should be melted in a skillet over medium-high heat. Add the mushrooms and season with salt. Cook, occasionally stirring, for 5 to 10 minutes or until the mushrooms are golden brown. There should be beef and onion added. Stir-fry the mixture for about 5 minutes until the meat is crumbly and browned and the onions are translucent. For seasoning, include cayenne and black pepper.

2. Add the flour and minced garlic, and cook for one minute. Vodka should be added and left to evaporate for about 30 seconds. Add water and beef broth while stirring, then simmer. Cook for 10 minutes while stirring occasionally.

3. Add noodles and reduce heat to medium. 5 minutes should be spent simmering with a tight-fitting lid on. Open the cover, then thoroughly stir. Recover the lid and continue cooking for 3 more minutes, or until the noodles are tender. (View the Cook's Note.)

4. Once the noodles are cooked, turn down the heat and stir in the sour cream. Top the dish immediately with more sour cream, green onions, or chives if desired.

114. Slow Cooker Beef Stew

Prep Time: 20 minutes

Cook Time: 4 hours

Total Time: 4 hours 20 minutes

Servings: 6

Ingredients

➢ Two lbs beef stew meat, cut into 1-inch pieces
➢ ¼ cups of all-purpose flour
➢ ½ tsp. salt
➢ ½ tsp. ground black pepper
➢ 1 ½ cups of beef broth
➢ 4 medium carrots, sliced

- ➢ 3 medium potatoes, diced
- ➢ 1 medium onion, diced
- ➢ 1 stalk celery, diced
- ➢ 1 tsp. Worcestershire sauce
- ➢ 1 tsp. ground paprika
- ➢ One clove of garlic, minced
- ➢ 1 large bay leaf

Directions

1. Ingredient gathering.
2. In a slow cooker, put the meat.
3. In a small bowl, combine flour, salt, and pepper. Stir the mixture after pouring it over the meat.
4. Stir together the beef broth, carrots, potatoes, onion, celery, Worcestershire sauce, paprika, and bay leaf before adding.
5. Cook the beef covered on Low for 8 to 12 hours or on High for 4 to 6 hours, or until it can be cut with a spoon.

115. Easy Meatloaf

Prep Time: 15 minutes

Cook Time: 1 hour

Total Time: 1 hour 15 minutes

Servings: 8

Ingredients

- ➢ 1 ½ lbs ground beef
- ➢ 1 egg

- ➢ One onion, diced
- ➢ 1 cup of milk
- ➢ 1 cup of dried bread crumbs
- ➢ salt and pepper to taste
- ➢ ⅓ cups of ketchup
- ➢ 2 tbsp. brown sugar
- ➢ 2 tbsp. prepared mustard

Directions

1. Oven: 350 degrees Fahrenheit (175 degrees C). Grease a 9x5-inch loaf pan just a little.
2. Combine the bread crumbs, milk, egg, onion, and ground beef in a sizable bowl and season with salt and pepper. Into the prepared loaf pan, transfer.
3. Spread ketchup, brown sugar, and mustard evenly over the top of the meatloaf after thoroughly combining them in a small bowl.
4. Bake in the preheated oven for about an hour until the center is no longer pink.

116. Beef Bulgogi

Prep Time: 10 minutes

Cook Time: 5 minutes

Additional Time: 1 hour

Total Time: 1 hour 15 minutes

Servings: 4

Ingredients

- ➤ 5 tbsp. soy sauce
- ➤ ¼ cups of diced green onion
- ➤ 2 ½ tbsp. white sugar
- ➤ 2 tbsp. minced garlic
- ➤ 2 tbsp. sesame seeds
- ➤ 2 tbsp. sesame oil
- ➤ ½ tsp. ground black pepper
- ➤ 1 lb flank steak, thinly sliced

Directions

1. Amass all the ingredients.
2. Combine pepper, sugar, sesame seeds, sesame oil, green onion, and soy sauce in a bowl.
3. In a small dish, arrange slices of flank steak. Overtop, pour marinade. Overnight or for at least one hour, cover and chill.
4. Lightly oil the grate and preheat an outdoor grill to high heat.
5. Slices of flank steak should be quickly grilled until slightly charred and cooked through, about 1 to 2 minutes per side.

117. Best Roast Beef

Prep Time: 5 minutes

Cook Time: 1 hour

Additional Time: 15 minutes

Total Time: 1 hour 20 minutes

Servings: 6

Ingredients

- ➤ 3 lbs beef eye of round roast at room temperature
- ➤ ½ tsp. kosher salt, or more to taste
- ➤ ½ tsp. garlic powder, or more to taste
- ➤ ¼ tsp. freshly ground black pepper or more to taste

Directions

1. Amass all the ingredients.
2. Bake at 375 degrees Fahrenheit (190 degrees C).
3. Ascertain that the roast is at room temperature. Tie the roast with cotton twine at 3-inch intervals to prevent drying out and promote more even cooking. In a baking pan, place the roast on a rack.
4. In a small bowl, combine pepper, garlic powder, and salt. Into the meat, rub the seasoning mixture.
5. Put the roast in the preheated oven for 60 minutes or 20 minutes per lb if your roast is larger or smaller. 120 to 125 degrees Fahrenheit should be displayed on an instant-read thermometer inserted in the center (49 to 52 degrees C).
6. Take out of the oven and place on a cutting board. Allow to rest, covered loosely with foil, for 15 to 20 minutes to allow juices to redistribute.
7. Slice and present.

118. Pork Tenderloin with Peaches

Prep Time: 15 minutes

Cook Time: 50 minutes

Total Time: 1 hour 5 minutes

Servings: 8

Ingredients

- Three slices bacon
- 1 (2 lb) package pork tenderloin
- ½ tsp. Salt
- ¼ tsp. Freshly ground black pepper
- ¾ tsp. ground ginger, divided
- 1 ½ cups of vertically sliced onion
- 1 ½ tsp. minced garlic
- 2 cups of peeled and sliced fresh peaches
- 1 cup of low-sodium chicken broth
- 2 tbsp. frozen orange juice concentrate
- 1 tsp. fish sauce
- 2 tbsp. water
- 2 tbsp. cornstarch
- fresh parsley for garnish

Directions

1. Add the bacon to a large skillet, and cook for about 10 minutes, turning it occasionally, until it is evenly browned and crisp. Bacon slices should be dried with paper towels. Keep the skillet drippings for later use.
2. Salt, pepper, and 1/4 tsp. Ground ginger is added to the pork tenderloin after it has been dried with paper towels.
3. Raising the heat to medium-high, brown the tenderloin for 5 to 7 minutes on each side in the bacon drippings. The

tenderloin has been removed from the skillet, transferred, and kept warm on a plate.

4. Heat to medium-low. Slices of onion should be added to the same skillet and stirred for three to five minutes, or until they are soft and starting to turn color. One minute later, add the garlic and stir until fragrant.

5. Sliced peaches, chicken broth, orange juice concentrate, and the last of the ground ginger should be added. Tenderloin is returned to the skillet after coming to a boil. Assemble peaches on top of the meat, cover, lower the heat to a simmer, and cook for 20 to 25 minutes, or until the pork is just barely pink in the center. The center should register at least 145 degrees Fahrenheit on an instant-read thermometer (63 degrees C).

6. On a serving platter, arrange the pork and the peaches.

7. In the meantime, combine fish sauce, water, and cornstarch in a small bowl and whisk to combine thoroughly. Turn the heat up to medium and re-boil the contents of the skillet. Stir quickly while adding the cornstarch mixture to the liquid in the skillet for about five minutes, or until the sauce is bubbling and thickened.

8. Put sauce on top of the pork and peaches. Sprinkle the peaches with crumbled cooked bacon. If desired, add some parsley to the garnish before serving.

119. Easy Marinated Pork Tenderloin

Prep Time: 5 minutes

Cook Time: 45 minutes

Additional Time: 1 hour

Total Time: 1 hour 50 minutes

Servings: 3

Ingredients

- ➤ ¼ cups of olive oil
- ➤ ¼ cups of soy sauce
- ➤ 1 clove garlic, minced
- ➤ 3 tbsp. dijon honey mustard
- ➤ salt and ground black pepper to taste
- ➤ 2 lbs pork tenderloin

Directions

1. Combine the olive oil, soy sauce, garlic, mustard, salt, and pepper in a bowl.
2. Put the marinade and the pork loin in a sizable resealable plastic bag. At least an hour before cooking, marinate in the refrigerator.
3. Set the oven to 350 degrees F. (175 degrees C).
4. After moving it to a baking dish, pour the marinade over the pork loin.
5. Cook in the preheated oven for 45 to 60 minutes, or until the center of the pork is no longer pink. 145 degrees Fahrenheit should be displayed on an instant-read thermometer inserted in the center (63 degrees C).

120. Crispy Pork Cutlets

Prep Time: 20 minutes

Cook Time: 30 minutes

Additional Time: 15 minutes

Total Time: 1 hour 5 minutes

Servings: 4

Ingredients

- 2 (1 1/4 lb) fully trimmed pork tenderloins, cut into 8 pieces
- salt and freshly ground black pepper to taste
- Two tbsp. all-purpose flour, or as needed
- 2 eggs, beaten
- 3 cups of panko bread crumbs
- 2 tbsp. butter
- ⅓ cups of diced dill pickles
- 1 jalapeno pepper, seeded and minced
- One bunch of green onions, diced, green tops reserved
- 1 pinch cayenne pepper, or to taste
- 1 ½ tbsp. all-purpose flour
- 1 ½ cups of cold milk, or more as needed
- 1 tsp. Worcestershire sauce, or to taste
- ¼ tsp. freshly ground black pepper or more to taste
- ½ cup of vegetable oil for frying
- salt to taste

Directions

1. Pork pieces should be placed on a stable, level surface between two sheets of heavy plastic (resealable freezer bags

work well). Use a meat mallet's smooth side to firmly lb pork until it is 1/2 inch thick.

2. Add 2 tbsp. Lightly coat both sides of flour, and transfer the pork pieces to a plate. Season both sides liberally with salt and black pepper. Pour the eggs over the pork and turn to coat.

3. Pork pieces should be coated on both sides after being placed in a shallow bowl with panko. Place the breaded cutlets on a clean plate, wrap them in plastic, and place it in the refrigerator for 15 minutes.

4. Over medium heat, melt butter in a skillet. Green onions, pickles, and jalapenos are added, cooked, and stirred for 3 minutes. Add 1 1/2 tbsp. Of flour, then cook and stir for 3 minutes.

5. 2 to 3 tbsp. Cold milk should be whisked in gradually. Add Worcestershire sauce, black pepper, and the remaining milk. For five minutes, simmer on low. Set sauce aside after flavoring and seasoning adjustments.

6. In a big skillet over medium-high heat, warm up 1/4 cup of vegetable oil. Add half of the breaded pork cutlets, and cook for 4 to 5 minutes per side until the pork is no longer pink inside and the crust is nicely browned.

7. Place on a plate covered with paper towels. Salt should be added. Use the remaining vegetable oil and pork cutlets to repeat.

8. Top cutlets with sauce before serving.

121. Asian Pork Tenderloin

Prep Time: 15 minutes

Cook Time: 25 minutes

Additional Time: 8 hours

Total Time: 8 hours 40 minutes

Servings: 4

Ingredients

- 1 (2 lb) fat-trimmed pork tenderloin
- ⅓ cups of lite soy sauce
- ¼ cups of sesame oil
- 2 tbsp. Worcestershire sauce
- Three green onions, diced
- Four cloves garlic, crushed
- 2 tbsp. packed light brown sugar
- 1 ½ tbsp. Asian chile paste
- 1 ½ tsp. pepper

Directions

1. In a shallow dish, place the pork tenderloin.
2. Put Worcestershire sauce, sesame oil, and soy sauce in a medium bowl. Once everything is combined, stir in the green onions, garlic, brown sugar, chile paste, and pepper. As you turn the tenderloin to coat it, pour sauce over it. The dish should be covered and marinated in the fridge for eight to twelve hours.
3. Set the oven to 450°F for preheating (230 degrees C).

4. Place the marinated pork tenderloin in a baking pan lined with aluminum foil.
5. Roast for 25 to 30 minutes in the preheated oven, or until an instant-read thermometer inserted in the center registers at least 145 degrees F (63 degrees C). Before carving, let the food sit for five to ten minutes.

122. Pork Stir Fry

Prep Time: 25 minutes

Cook Time: 15 minutes

Total Time: 40 minutes

Servings: 6

Ingredients

➢ 5 tbsp. reduced-sodium soy sauce
➢ 2 tbsp. rice wine vinegar
➢ 1 tbsp. cornstarch
➢ 2 tbsp. sesame oil divided
➢ 1 (1 lb) pork tenderloin, cut into strips
➢ One fresh red chile pepper, diced
➢ Two cloves garlic, minced
➢ One onion, diced
➢ One green bell pepper, diced
➢ One head bok choy, leaves and stalks separated, diced
➢ Two crowns of broccoli, diced
➢ 1 tsp. ground ginger

Directions

1. Combine the soy sauce, vinegar, and cornstarch in a small bowl.
2. In a wok over medium-high heat, warm 1 tbsp. Of sesame oil. Tenderloin strips should be cooked and stirred in hot oil for 2 to 4 minutes or until barely browned. After removing the pork to a plate, re-heat the wok.
3. Cook and stir red chile pepper and garlic in hot oil until sizzling, about 15 to 30 seconds after adding the last of the sesame oil to the wok. Cook and stir the onion and bell pepper for 2 to 3 minutes or until the onion softens. Bok choy stalks that have been diced are added to the onion mixture and cooked and stirred for three minutes.
4. Add the broccoli to the wok and stir-fry for 2 minutes or until just tender. Cook and stir until everything is thoroughly combined before adding the diced bok choy leaves and the pork. Ginger is used to seasoning the pork mixture. It is cooked and stirred for 5 to 7 minutes or until the broccoli is soft.

123. Pork Steaks

Prep Time: 15 minutes

Cook Time: 30 minutes

Total Time: 45 minutes

Servings: 6

Ingredients

- ¼ cups of butter
- ¼ cups of soy sauce
- One bunch of green onions, diced
- Two cloves garlic, minced
- Six pork butt steaks

Directions

1. Stir soy sauce into butter as it is melting in a skillet over medium heat. Cook for about 2 minutes, stirring occasionally, before adding the green onions and garlic.
2. Put the pork steaks in the pan. Cook each side for 8 to 10 minutes under a cover until browned. When the thickest part of the steak registers 145 degrees F (63 degrees C), which takes about 10 minutes, remove the lid and continue cooking.

124. Pork Carnitas

Prep Time: 15 minutes

Cook Time: 3 hours 30 minutes

Total Time: 3 hours 45 minutes

Servings: 12

Ingredients

- ¼ cups of vegetable oil
- 4 lbs pork shoulder, cut into several large pieces
- 3 tbsp. kosher salt

- One onion, diced
- 1 clove garlic, crushed
- 3 tbsp. lime juice
- 1 tbsp. chili powder
- ½ tsp. dried oregano
- ½ tsp. ground cumin
- 4 (14.5 Oz.) cans of chicken broth

Directions

1. Amass all the ingredients.
2. Vegetable oil is heated in a large Dutch oven over high heat. Before adding the pork shoulder pieces to the Dutch oven, salt them. Cook for 10 minutes or until everything is golden brown.
3. Add the cumin, onion, garlic, lime juice, chili powder, herbs, and spices. Bring to a boil after adding the chicken broth. Simmer for about 2 1/2 hours, with the heat reduced to medium-low, with the lid on.
4. Oven: 400 degrees Fahrenheit (200 degrees C).
5. The pork shoulder should be moved to a big baking sheet with the cooking liquid saved. Sprinkle the pork pieces with a little of the cooking liquid and salt them very sparingly.
6. For about 30 minutes, brown the pork in the preheated oven. Every ten minutes, add more cooking liquid; as the pork browns, shred it with two forks.

125. Crispy Pork Carnitas

Prep Time: 15 minutes

Cook Time: 3 hours 40 minutes

Total Time: 3 hours 55 minutes

Servings: 6

Ingredients

- ➢ 3 lbs boneless pork butt
- ➢ 8 cloves garlic, peeled
- ➢ ¼ cups of olive oil
- ➢ 1 orange, juiced, orange parts of peel removed and sliced into thin strips
- ➢ 1 tbsp. kosher salt
- ➢ 2 bay leaves, torn in half
- ➢ 1 tsp. ground black pepper
- ➢ 1 tsp. ground cumin
- ➢ ¾ tsp. ground cinnamon
- ➢ ½ tsp. Chinese 5-spice powder

Directions

1. Achieve a 275°F oven temperature (135 degrees C).
2. Trim the pork fat, dice the meat into 2-inch cubes, and roughly chop the fat.
3. Pork meat and fat are combined with garlic, olive oil, orange peel, orange juice, salt, bay leaves, black pepper, cumin, cinnamon, and five-spice powder in a sizable bowl. The mixture is continued until the pork is thoroughly coated. The mixture should be placed in a 9x13-inch baking dish. Place the dish on a baking sheet and tightly wrap it in aluminum foil.

4. For about 3 1/2 hours, bake the pork in a preheated oven until it is tender to the fork.
5. Preheat the oven's broiler while positioning an oven rack about 6 inches from the heat source.
6. Take out the bay leaves, orange peel, and garlic from the baking dish. Pork should be placed in a colander over a bowl. Over the pork, pour any accumulated juices from the baking dish. Add some of the accumulated juices to replace the pork in the baking dish.
7. 3 minutes of cooking time under the preheated broiler. Drizzle more accumulated juices over the pork and continue broiling until crispy, 3 to 5 minutes. Put the pork on a serving plate and pour any remaining accumulated juices over it.

Chapter 7: Cakes, Cookies, and Dessert Recipes

126. Baked Churro Bites

Prep Time: 30 minutes

Cook Time: 40 minutes

Cool Time: 10 minutes

Total Time: 1 hour 40 minutes

Servings: 30

Ingredients

- ➢ 1 1/4 cups of water
- ➢ 5 tbsp. cold unsalted butter
- ➢ Two packed tbsp. brown sugar
- ➢ 1/2 tsp. salt
- ➢ 1 1/4 cups of all-purpose flour
- ➢ 1 tsp. vanilla extract
- ➢ Two large eggs
- ➢ 2 tbsp. melted butter for brushing on before sugaring
- ➢ cooking spray

Cinnamon Sugar:

- ➢ One/Three cups of white sugar
- ➢ 1 tbsp. cinnamon
- ➢ 1/4 tsp. salt

Directions

1. Bring water, butter, brown sugar, and salt to a simmer in a saucepan over medium heat. All of the flour should be added at once. Cook, constantly stirring, until a soft, sticky dough ball forms and a starchy film covers the pan's bottom, about 5 minutes.
2. Cook for an additional minute while stirring and scraping any film on the bottom of the pan. The bottom surface won't be completely clean, but the dough will reabsorb some.
3. After transferring, allow cooling in a bowl for ten minutes.

4. Using a spatula, gradually add the vanilla extract and eggs. The mixture will initially separate but smear together into a sticky dough.
5. Oven: 425 degrees Fahrenheit (220 degrees C). Silpat mats or parchment paper should be used to line 2 baking sheets.
6. Fill a pastry bag with a star-tipped pastry bag with the dough (I used a number 356 tip). Place 3 to 4-inch ropes, spaced a few inches apart, on the baking sheets that have been prepared. "cut" through the dough with the back of a knife at the end of each pipe to create a clean end. Pipe 14 to 15 churros per baking sheet, as this recipe yields 28 to 30 bite-sized churros.
7. Once piped, liberally mist the tops of the churros with vegetable oil spray before dousing the entire pan with water.
8. Cook in the oven for 20 to 25 minutes or until the churros are puffy and the edges are browned. To vent the heat, turn off the oven and leave the door open for about 10 seconds. Churros should rest in the oven for 10 minutes before closing the door, leaving a small gap of 8 to 12 inches.
9. Then, working in six batches at a time, brush them lightly with melted butter before tossing them in a bag of cinnamon sugar to coat.

127. Samoa Cookie Bars

Prep Time: 30 minutes

Cook Time: 20 minutes

Cool Time: 1 hour

Total Time: 1 hour 50 minutes

Servings: 24

Ingredients

- ➢ cooking spray
- ➢ 1 ½ cups of flour
- ➢ 1 tbsp. cornstarch
- ➢ ½ tsp. baking powder
- ➢ ½ tsp. salt
- ➢ ½ cup of softened butter
- ➢ ¼ cups of white sugar
- ➢ ¼ cups of packed brown sugar
- ➢ 1 large egg yolk
- ➢ 1 tsp. vanilla extract
- ➢ 1 (13.4 Oz.) can dulce de leche
- ➢ 3 tbsp. milk
- ➢ 1 (14 Oz.) package of sweetened flaked coconut
- ➢ 1 (12 Oz.) bag of semisweet chocolate chips divided

Directions

1. Set the oven to 350 degrees Fahrenheit (175 degrees C). Line a 9x13-inch baking pan using foil, extending foil over the edges. Apply cooking spray to foil.
2. In a small bowl, mash the flour, cornflour, baking soda, and salt to make the crust.
3. Beat butter in a sizable bowl for 30 seconds at medium speed using an electric mixer. Add both sugars and beat at a medium-high speed until fluffy and light. Add vanilla extract

and egg yolk after mixing. Blend in the flour mixture (the mixture will be crumbly). On the bottom of the prepared pan, press the dough.

4. Bake crust in the oven for 10 to 12 minutes or until edges are light brown.
5. In the meantime, combine milk and dulce de leche in a medium bowl. Add coconut flakes and stir.
6. When the chocolate has melted, sprinkle 1 1/2 cups of chocolate chips over the hot crust and let stand for 5 minutes. The melted chocolate should be evenly layered on the crust. Spread the coconut mixture over the chocolate layer with care. Back in the oven, bake for an additional 10 minutes. On a wire rack, allow the pan to cool.
7. The remaining chocolate chips should be heated in a small bowl for 30 to 45 seconds, stirring once halfway through. Put melted chocolate on top of the coconut mixture. They were covered and chilled for about an hour or until set. Lift out uncut cookies using foil. Into bars; cut.

128. Maple Cups of cakes

Prep Time: 15 minutes

Cook Time: 20 minutes

Total Time: 35 minutes

Servings: 24

Ingredients

- 1 cup of maple syrup
- 5 tbsp. margarine
- One large egg
- 1 ½ cups of all-purpose flour
- ½ cup of whole wheat flour
- Two ¼ tsp. baking powder
- ½ tsp. ground nutmeg
- ½ tsp. salt
- ¼ tsp. ground ginger
- ½ cup of milk

Directions

1. Oven: 350 degrees Fahrenheit (175 degrees C). Butter two 12-cups of muffin tins.
2. Margarine and maple syrup should be thoroughly combined and creamy in a large bowl. Add egg, blending well.
3. Mix the all-purpose and whole wheat flour in a small bowl with the baking powder, salt, ginger, and nutmeg. Batch-wise, alternately adds milk and the dry ingredients to the wet ingredients, beating the batter just long enough after each addition. The mixture should be poured into the muffin cups halfway.
4. Bake for 20 to 30 minutes in the oven or until a toothpick inserted in the center comes out clean.

129. Homemade Tagalongs

Prep Time: 30 minutes

Cook Time: 7 minutes

Chill Time: 1 hour

Stand Time: 1 hour

Total Time: 2 hours 37 minutes

Servings: 46

Ingredients

- ➤ 1 cup of butter, softened
- ➤ ¾ cups of white sugar
- ➤ ½ tsp. salt
- ➤ Two large egg yolks
- ➤ 2 tsp. vanilla extract
- ➤ 2 cups of flour
- ➤ 1 cup of powdered sugar
- ➤ 1 cup of peanut butter
- ➤ ½ cup of heavy cream
- ➤ 8 Oz. milk chocolate, diced
- ➤ 8 Oz. chocolate-flavor candy coating, diced

Directions

1. With an electric mixer set to medium speed, beat butter in a large bowl for 30 seconds. Mix in the salt and sugar after adding them. Combine vanilla and egg yolks. As dough forms, gradually add flour. About an hour of covered chilling will make the dough manageable.
2. Set the oven to 375°F for preheating (190 degrees C).
3. Roll out the dough to a 1/4-inch thickness on a lightly dusted surface. If necessary, reroll dough scraps before

cutting the dough with a 2-inch cookie cutter. On an ungreased biscuit sheet, space the cutouts 2 inches apart.

4. Bake in a preheated oven for 7 to 8 minutes or until golden brown. Transfer to a wire rack to finish cooling.

5. Powdered sugar, peanut butter, and cream should be combined separately. Each cookie's center should be slightly mounded after being spread with 2 tsp. On wax paper, arrange.

6. In the interim, set up a wire rack on wax paper. Melt the milk chocolate and candy coating in a small saucepan over low heat. Cover cookies with a spoon, letting the extra drip off. Set aside to stand on the prepared rack.

130. Mocha Cookie Bars

Prep Time: 15 minutes

Cook Time: 20 minutes

Cool Time: 10 minutes

Total Time: 45 minutes

Servings: 16

Ingredients

- ➤ 1 tbsp. instant espresso powder
- ➤ 1 tbsp. strong brewed coffee
- ➤ One cup of all-purpose flour
- ➤ ¼ cup of unsweetened cocoa powder
- ➤ ½ tsp. Cream of tartar

- ➤ ½ tsp. baking soda
- ➤ ½ tsp. salt
- ➤ ¼ tsp. ground cinnamon
- ➤ ½ cups of unsalted butter softened
- ➤ ½ cups of white sugar
- ➤ ¼ cups of firmly packed brown sugar
- ➤ One large egg at room temperature
- ➤ 2 tsp. vanilla extract

Topping:

- ➤ 1 tbsp. white sugar
- ➤ ½ tsp. ground cinnamon

Directions

1. Oven: 350 degrees Fahrenheit (175 degrees C). Line an 8x8-inch square pan with parchment paper to have an overhang on all sides.
2. Espresso powder should completely dissolve after being mixed with coffee in a small bowl.
3. In a bowl, combine the flour, cocoa, baking soda, salt, cream of tartar, and 1/4 tsp. Cinnamon.
4. In a bowl, use an electric mixer to beat the butter, 1/2 cup of white sugar, and brown sugar until they are light and fluffy. The espresso mixture, egg, and vanilla should all be thoroughly combined. Add the flour mixture and mix just until a dough starts to form. Press the dough firmly and uniformly into the prepared pan using lightly dusted hands.
5. In a small bowl, combine 1 tbsp: of white sugar and the final 1/2 tsp. of cinnamon. Sprinkle the sugar mixture over the dough in an even layer.

6. Bake in the oven for 20 to 23 minutes or until the dough in the pan's center feels barely set.
7. Give cookies 10 minutes to cool in the pan. Cookies can be transferred to a wire rack using the dangling parchment, then completely cooled before being cut into bars.

131. S'mores Cookies

Prep Time: 30 minutes

Cook Time: 7 minutes

Chill Time: 1 hour

Total Time: 1 hour 37 minutes

Servings: 36

Ingredients

➢ ⅓ cups of milk
➢ ¼ cups of honey
➢ 1 tbsp. vanilla extract
➢ 2 cups of all-purpose flour
➢ ¾ cups of packed brown sugar
➢ ½ cup of whole-wheat flour
➢ 1 tsp. baking soda
➢ ½ tsp. salt
➢ ½ cup of cold butter

Marshmallow Icing:

➢ ½ (7 Oz.) jar marshmallow creme

- ➢ 1 cup of powdered sugar
- ➢ 2 tbsp. butter softened
- ➢ 3 tbsp. Milk, or more as needed

Chocolate Icing:

- ➢ 12 Oz. milk chocolate, diced
- ➢ 2 tsp. vegetable shortening

Directions

1. Combine honey, vanilla extract, and 1/3 cup of milk in a small bowl. Combine all-purpose flour, brown sugar, whole-wheat flour, baking soda, and salt in a large bowl. Using a pastry blender, mix ingredients until they resemble coarse crumbs. Add 1/2 cup of cold butter—just enough milk mixture to combine after adding. When forming a ball, gently knead the mixture. Cut the dough into four pieces. After chilling for about an hour to make it easy to handle, wrap each portion in plastic wrap.

2. Three hundred fifty degrees Fahrenheit should be set for the oven (175 degrees C).

3. Roll one portion of the dough into a 6-inch square on a surface lightly dusted with flour—squares of two inches, cut. On an ungreased biscuit sheet, spread out 1 inch apart. Use a fork to prick—7 to 9 minutes of baking time or until edges are firm. Discard; let cool on a wire rack. Continue with the remaining dough.

4. Combine marshmallow creme, powdered sugar, and two tbsp. Of butter in a bowl to make the marshmallow icing. To achieve dipping consistency, stir in just enough milk. Dip

cookies in icing and let extra drip off. Arrange on wire racks placed over wax paper and wait until they are set.

5. To make the chocolate icing, melt the chocolate and shortening in a small bowl in the microwave for about 90 seconds, stirring twice. Each biscuit should receive about 1 tbsp of melted chocolate to coat. When ready, let stand on a wire rack placed over wax paper.

6. Regarding sandwiches, Put marshmallow icing on one side of the biscuit. Sandwich cookies with icing sides facing in, dipping one side of each in chocolate icing. Set aside.

7. To make half-and-half cookies, dip each biscuit in the chocolate and marshmallow icing alternately. Set aside.

132. Snickerdoodle Bars

Prep Time: 10 minutes

Cook Time: 20 minutes

Cool Time: 1 hour

Total Time: 1 hour 30 minutes

Servings: 16

Ingredients

- ½ cup of unsalted butter softened
- ½ cup of white sugar
- ¼ cups of firmly packed brown sugar
- One large egg at room temperature
- 2 tsp. vanilla extract

- One ¼ cup of all-purpose flour
- ½ tsp. cream of tartar
- ½ tsp. baking soda
- ½ tsp. salt
- ¼ tsp. the ground cinnamon divided
- ⅛ tsp. ground nutmeg

Topping:

- 1 tbsp. white sugar
- ½ tsp. ground cinnamon

Directions

1. Oven: 350 degrees Fahrenheit (175 degrees C). Line an 8x8-inch square pan with parchment paper to have an overhang on all sides.
2. In a bowl, use an electric mixer to beat butter, 1/2 cup of white sugar, and brown sugar until fluffy. Add egg and vanilla, blending well after each addition. When a dough starts to take shape, add the flour, cream of tartar, salt, baking soda, 1/4 tsp—cinnamon, and nutmeg.
3. Into the prepared pan, put the dough. Put some flour on your hands and press the dough into the bottom of the pan evenly and firmly.
4. 1 tbsp. White sugar and 1/2 tsp. Cinnamon should be combined in a small bowl. Over the dough, evenly sprinkle.
5. Place pan in the preheated oven, and bake for 20 to 23 minutes, or until the dough feels barely set in the center of the pan. Never overbake.

6. Allow the cookies to cool in the pan for 10 minutes before removing them to a wire rack to finish cooling. Cut sixteen bars, please.

133. Mom-Mom Kolar's Chocolate Rum Pie

Prep Time: 20 minutes

Cook Time: 25 minutes

Additional Time: 3 hours

Total Time: 3 hours 45 minutes

Servings: 8

Ingredients
For chocolate-rum filling

- ½ cup of white sugar
- 1 (.25 Oz.) envelope of unflavored gelatin
- 1 pinch salt
- 1 cup of whole milk
- Two large egg yolks
- 1 (6 Oz.) package of semisweet chocolate chips
- .3 cups of dark rum

For the whipped cream mixture

- ¼ cups of sugar
- 1 cup of heavy whipping cream

- ➤ 1 tsp. vanilla extract
- ➤ 1 (9-inch) pie shell, baked

Directions

1. Gelatin, salt, and 1/2 cup of sugar are combined in a saucepan. Add milk and yolks to one egg. Over low heat, stir and cook for 3 to 5 minutes or until slightly thickened. Delete from the heat, then stir in the chocolate pieces until smooth. Stir in the rum after you've added it. It takes about an hour to set partially.
2. Egg whites should be electrically mixed-blended until soft peaks form in a chilled glass or metal bowl. While beating, gradually add 1/4 cup of sugar until stiff peaks form. Add egg whites and combine with the chocolate mixture.
3. Combine the cream and vanilla extract in a chilled glass or metal bowl and beat with an electric mixer until stiff peaks form. The whipped cream and chocolate mixture are added in layers to the pie crust. To marbelize, twirl the top with a fork.
4. The pie should be refrigerated for 1 to 2 hours or until firm.

134. Cherry Crunch Dessert

Prep Time: 15 minutes

Bake Time: 20 minutes

Additional Time: 15 minutes

Total Time: 50 minutes

Servings: 16

Ingredients
Crust:

- 1 ½ cups of all-purpose flour
- 2 tbsp. white sugar
- ½ tsp. salt
- ¾ cups of softened butter
- 1 cup of diced pecans

Filling:

- 2 cups of confectioners' sugar
- One (8 Oz.) package of cream cheese, softened
- 1 (12 Oz.) container of frozen whipped topping, thawed
- 1 tsp. Vanilla bean paste

Topping:

- 2 (21 Oz.) cans of cherry pie filling

Directions

1. Oven: 350 degrees Fahrenheit (175 degrees C).
2. Combine the flour, sugar, and salt in a medium bowl. Use a pastry blender, fork, or fingers to crumble in the butter, then add the pecans. Press the crust mixture evenly into a 9x13-inch baking pan that has not been greased.
3. For about 20 minutes in a preheated oven, bake the crust until golden. Decrease heat.
4. In the meantime, combine cream cheese and confectioners' sugar in a big bowl. Whipping cream that has been thawed is added, followed by vanilla bean paste.

5. Spread cherry pie filling over the cream cheese filling-coated crust after it has cooled. When ready to serve, keep chilled.

135. Spotted Dick

Cook Time: 1 hour 30 minutes

Active Time: 30 minutes

Cool Time: 1 hour 40 minutes

Total Time: 3 hours 40 minutes

Servings: 6

Ingredients
Custard Sauce

- ½ cup of whole milk
- ½ cup of heavy whipping cream
- ⅛ tsp. kosher salt
- ¼ cups of granulated sugar
- Two large egg yolks
- 1 tsp. vanilla extract

Pudding

- One ⅔ cup of all-purpose flour
- 2 ½ tsp. baking powder
- ½ tsp. kosher salt
- 7 tbsp. cold unsalted butter, cubed, plus more for greasing bowl and parchment
- ⅓ cups of granulated sugar

- ⅓ cups of dried currants
- ⅓ cups of raisins
- 1 tsp. grated lemon zest
- ⅔ cups of whole milk
- 1 tsp. vanilla extract

Directions

1. Heat the milk, cream, and salt in a saucepan over medium-low heat while frequently stirring until steaming.
2. In a bowl, thoroughly combine the sugar and egg yolks. Pour half of the warm milk mixture into the egg yolk mixture while whisking continuously. Re-whisk the egg yolk mixture into the milk mixture in the pan. Stirring constantly, cook egg yolk mixture over medium-low for 3 to 5 minutes, or until it barely thickens and coats the back of a spoon (see Cook's Note).
3. Add vanilla extract after removing from the heat. In a bowl, pour the egg yolk mixture through a fine mesh sieve; leave it to cool for 30 minutes at room temperature, uncovered. Put a loose cover on it and chill for about an hour or until completely cold.
4. Prepare a 1.5-quart heat-resistant metal bowl with butter while the custard sauce cools. Draw a circle on a piece of parchment paper, cut it out, and use it to line the bottom of the bowl.
5. In a sizable bowl, stir together the flour, baking soda, and salt. Till the mixture resembles coarse breadcrumbs, manually or with a pastry blender, cut the butter into the flour mixture. Once everything is thoroughly combined, add

sugar, currants, raisins, and lemon zest. Just until combined, slowly stir in milk and vanilla. It will be a very thick batter.

6. Smooth the batter into an even layer as you pour it into the prepared bowl. A piece of parchment paper buttered should cover the bowl loosely. Double-layer aluminum foil should be used to cover the bowl tightly. Aluminum foil should be tightly wrapped twice around the top edge of the bowl with kitchen twine to keep it in place. A handle can be made by tying another piece of string to the twine on either side of the bowl.

7. Create a perforated platform in a big, deep pot by placing an expandable metal steamer basket on its side. About 1 inch of water should be in the pot. Over medium-high heat, bring to a boil. Then, lower the heat to a simmer. Add the bowl to the pot. Steam the custard with the cover on until it is set, and a wooden pick inserted in the center comes out clean for one hour and thirty minutes to an hour and forty minutes. An instant-read thermometer in the middle reads around 180 degrees Fahrenheit (82 degrees C). Increase the heat to maintain a simmer, and add more water as necessary.

8. Utilizing the twine handle, carefully remove the bowl from the pot; then, take out and discard the twine, aluminum foil, and parchment paper. Allow the bowl to cool for 10 minutes.

9. Turn custard over onto a serving plate; take out the bowl and throw away the parchment. With chilled custard sauce, serve warm.

136. Coconut Bundt Cake

Prep Time: 30 minutes

Cook Time: 1 hour 30 minutes

Additional Time: 10 minutes

Total Time: 2 hours 10 minutes

Servings: 16

Ingredients
Cake

- 1 cup of butter, softened
- 1 cup of sour cream
- 3 cups of white sugar
- Six large eggs
- 1 tsp. coconut extract
- 1 tsp. vanilla extract
- 3 cups of all-purpose flour
- ½ tsp. baking powder
- 2 cups of flaked coconut
- 1 cup of white chocolate chips

Frosting

- 1 (4 Oz.) package of cream cheese, softened
- ¼ cups of softened butter
- 1 tsp. vanilla extract
- 2 cups of confectioners' sugar
- ¾ cups of flaked coconut, toasted

Directions

1. Oven: 325 degrees Fahrenheit (165 degrees C). Prepare a 10-inch tube pan with oil and flour.

2. Thoroughly combine the butter and sour cream in a big bowl using an electric mixer. Beat until light after adding sugar. One at a time beat well before adding the eggs. Vanilla and coconut extracts should be blended in. Flour and baking powder are added, then coconut flakes and white chocolate chips are folded. Fill the prepared pan with batter.

3. Bake for about one hour and 30 minutes in the oven or until a toothpick inserted in the center comes out clean. After 10 minutes of standing, invert the pan onto a cooling rack and trim the edges with a knife. Allow cool

ing.

4. Use an electric mixer to cream the cream cheese, butter, and vanilla extract in a big bowl. Add confectioners' sugar gradually until the frosting is smooth. Top the cake with toasted coconut flakes after frosting it.

137. Tom Cruise Cake

Prep Time: 45 minutes

Cook Time: 1 hour 10 minutes

Cool Time: 2 hours 50 minutes

Total Time: 4 hours 45 minutes

Servings: 12

Ingredients
Cake:

- 3 cups of cake flour
- 1 ½ tsp. baking powder
- ¾ tsp. salt
- ⅛ tsp. ground nutmeg
- ½ cup of unsalted butter softened
- 1 ½ cups of white sugar
- Two large eggs at room temperature
- Two large egg whites
- 1 tbsp. vanilla extract
- ½ tsp. almond extract
- 1 (13.5 Oz.) can of full-fat unsweetened coconut milk, thoroughly shaken
- One ¼ cup of sour cream at room temperature
- 1 cup of sweetened shredded coconut
- 1 cup of finely diced white chocolate

Frosting:

- 2 cups of sweetened shredded coconut
- ¼ cups of unsalted butter softened
- 1 (8 Oz.) package of cream cheese at room temperature
- 1 tsp. vanilla extract
- 1 pinch salt
- 2 ½ cups of powdered sugar
- 2 tbsp. heavy cream

Directions

1. Oven: 350 degrees Fahrenheit (175 degrees C). In a 12-cup of Bundt pan, grease and flour it.
2. Fluff, baking powder, salt, and nutmeg should all be combined.
3. Cream butter and sugar with an electric mixer until fluffy in a large bowl. One whole egg should be added at a time, beating well after each addition. Egg whites are added; beat for three minutes at medium-high speed. Add vanilla and almond extracts together. Add the coconut milk and continue beating until fully incorporated. Just combine after adding half of the flour mixture. Sour cream can now be added. Mix just until combined. Just combine after adding the remaining flour mixture. Add the white chocolate and coconut shreds by folding.
4. Once the batter is in the pan, gently tap it on the counter a few times to eliminate air bubbles.
5. For 60 to 70 minutes, or until a toothpick inserted into the center of the cake emerges with a few moist crumbs, bake in the preheated oven. Twenty minutes should pass while the cake cools in the pan before being removed to a wire rack to finish cooling.
6. Pour 2 cups of coconut flakes into a sizable, dry skillet. Stir continuously over medium-low heat for 3 to 4 minutes or until the coconut flakes start turning slightly blonde. Cool completely after removing from the pan.
7. Using an electric mixer, smooth out 1/4 cup of butter in a big bowl. Beat until fully combined after adding cream cheese. Salt and vanilla extract are combined. Add the

powdered sugar to one cup at a time while mixing well after each addition. Heavy cream should be added, then beaten for two minutes at medium-high speed.

8. After the cake has cooled, top it with dollops of frosting and spread it evenly around the top and sides. On the cake's top and sides, scatter-cooled, toasted coconut. Before serving, let the cake cool in the refrigerator for 30 minutes for the best results.

138. Peanut Butter M&M Cookies

Prep Time: 10 minutes

Cook Time: 10 minutes

Cool Time: 10 minutes

Total Time: 30 minutes

Servings: 16

Ingredients

- ➤ 1 cup of creamy peanut butter
- ➤ ¾ cups of firmly packed brown sugar
- ➤ 2 tbsp. firmly packed brown sugar
- ➤ One large egg at room temperature
- ➤ 1 tsp. baking soda
- ➤ 1 ½ tsp. vanilla extract
- ➤ ¼ tsp. salt
- ➤ ⅛ tsp. ground nutmeg
- ➤ ½ cup of mini candy-coated chocolate pieces

Directions

1. Oven: 350 degrees Fahrenheit (175 degrees C). Put parchment paper on two baking trays.
2. The following ingredients should be combined: peanut butter, 3/4 cups plus 2 tbsp—of brown sugar, egg, baking soda, vanilla, salt, and nutmeg. Add the M&M chocolate minis.
3. Place dough balls on the baking sheets spaced 1 inch apart, each measuring 1 1/2 tbsp in size. Roll out dough balls until they are about 1/2 inch thick.
4. For about 10 minutes, or until the tops of the cookies start to crack slightly, bake in the preheated oven. On the baking sheets, let the cookies cool for ten minutes before transferring them to a wire rack to finish cooling.

139. Peanut Butter Whipped Cream

Prep Time: 5 minutes

Total Time: 5 minutes

Servings: 8

Ingredients

- 2 cups of heavy whipping cream
- 1 cup of powdered sugar
- ⅓ cups of creamy peanut butter
- ½ tsp. vanilla extract

Directions

1. Mix cream, powdered sugar, peanut butter, and vanilla in a bowl.
2. Beat with an electric mixer at high speed for one to two minutes or until stiff peaks form.
3. Maintain in the fridge.

140. Chocolate Pistachio Cheesecake

Prep Time: 1 hour

Cook Time: 40 minutes

Stand Time: 6 hours

Total Time: 7 hours 40 minutes

Servings: 8

Ingredients

- 13 Oz. chocolate wafer cookies
- ¾ cups of raw unsalted pistachios, divided, plus more for garnish
- 2 tbsp. granulated sugar
- 2 tbsp. butter, melted
- 2 (8 Oz.) packages of reduced-fat cream cheese, softened
- 1 avocado, peeled, seeded, and mashed until smooth (1/2 cup)
- 2 cups of fat-free plain Greek-style yogurt
- 2 tbsp. cornstarch
- ¾ cups of granulated sugar

- Two large egg whites
- 1 tsp. almond extract
- ⅛ tsp. salt
- ¼ cups of whipping cream
- 2 tbsp. powdered sugar
- 1 tsp. vanilla extract
- 1 (16 Oz.) container of frozen nondairy low-fat whipped topping, thawed, plus more for garnish

Directions

1. Oven: 325 degrees Fahrenheit (165 degrees C). Use cooking spray to coat a 9-inch springform pan.
2. Cookies, 2 tbsp. Sugar and 1/4 cup of pistachios are processed in a food processor until mostly finely ground. It's acceptable to leave some texture. Pulse to combine after adding melted butter. Spread the mixture evenly in the prepared pan, then firmly press it into the bottom.
3. For pistachio butter, process the remaining 1/2 cup of pistachios in a small food processor for about 5 minutes or until very smooth and loose in consistency. Combine pistachio butter with cream cheese, avocado, 1 cup of yogurt, cornflour, and 3/4 cup of white sugar in a big bowl. Use a medium-speed electric mixer to beat until the mixture is nearly smooth. Add egg whites, almond flavoring, and a dash of salt; mix until combined. Dispense over the prepared crust.
4. Bake for about 40 minutes or until the surface near the edges seems set when gently jiggled. Cut the oven off. Oven time: 30 minutes for the cheesecake to stand. In the pan, cool for 15 minutes on a wire rack. Use a thin metal spatula

to remove the cheesecake from the pan's sides. Completely cool.

5. For the mousse, use an electric mixer to beat whipping cream, sugar, vanilla, the remaining 1 cup of yogurt, and a dash of salt in a bowl for about 4 minutes or until fluffy. Cover cheesecake with this.

6. Cover the mousse with whipped topping. For up to 5 days, refrigerate covered for at least 4 hours. Remove from pan, slice, and top with more whipped topping and pistachios to serve.

141. Eggnog Custard

Prep Time: 10 minutes

Cook Time: 35 minutes

Total Time: 45 minutes

Servings: 2

Ingredients

- ➢ One egg, beaten
- ➢ 1 cup of eggnog
- ➢ 2 tbsp. white sugar
- ➢ Two pinches of ground nutmeg

Directions

1. Oven: 350 degrees Fahrenheit (175 degrees C). One inch of water should be placed in an 8x8-inch baking dish.

2. In a bowl, combine the egg, eggnog, and sugar. Dispense into two small baking dishes. Add nutmeg to the tops. In the water-filled dish, put the baking dishes. If additional water is required, pour it until it reaches halfway up the sides of the smaller baking dishes.
3. Bake in a preheated oven for 35 to 45 minutes or until the tops are set. Cool before serving.

142. German Chocolate Cups of cakes

Cook Time: 5 minutes

Active Time: 45 minutes

Bake Time: 25 minutes

Cool Time: 1 hour 40 minutes

Total Time: 1 hour 55 minutes

Servings: 12

Ingredients
Coconut Icing

> - 1 (12 Oz.) can evaporate milk
> - ½ cup of unsalted butter
> - ⅓ cups of packed light brown sugar
> - ⅓ cups of granulated sugar
> - Three large egg yolks
> - ¼ tsp. table salt
> - ¾ cups of sweetened shredded coconut

- ¾ cups of toasted diced pecans or walnuts
- ½ tsp. almond extract

Cups of cakes

- baking spray with flour
- 1 ½ cups of all-purpose flour
- 1 ½ cups of granulated sugar
- ¾ cups of unsweetened cocoa (such as Hershey's)
- 1 tsp. instant espresso granules
- 1 tsp. baking powder
- ½ tsp. baking soda
- ¼ tsp. table salt
- ¾ cups of sour cream
- ½ cup of canola oil or other neutral oil
- ½ cup of whole buttermilk
- 2 tsp. vanilla extract
- Two large eggs at room temperature

Chocolate Frosting

- 10 tbsp. unsalted butter softened
- ⅓ cups of powdered sugar
- 3 tbsp. unsweetened cocoa
- ⅓ cups of 60% cacao dark chocolate chips, melted, cooled slightly
- ⅓ cups of heavy cream at room temperature
- ¾ tsp. vanilla extract

Directions
Coconut Icing:

1. Mix the egg yolks, brown sugar, butter, evaporated milk, and sugar in a saucepan. Cook for 3 to 4 minutes, stirring continuously, over medium-high heat or until the back of a spoon is coated. Add coconut, pecans, and almond extract after removing from heat. Transfer to a medium bowl, and cool until just chilled in the refrigerator, uncovered, occasionally stirring, for about an hour.

Cups of cakes:

1. Oven: 400 degrees Fahrenheit (200 degrees C). Paper liners should be used to line a 12-cup of the muffin pan. Baking spray should be used sparingly.
2. Combine the flour, granulated sugar, cocoa, espresso powder, baking soda, salt, and baking powder in a sizable bowl. Combine the sour cream, oil, buttermilk, vanilla, and eggs until smooth. Each muffin cup should receive about 1/3 cup of batter, distributed evenly.
3. When the oven is ready, put the pan inside and immediately lower the temperature to 350 degrees F. (175 degrees C).
4. Bake the cups of cakes for about 25 minutes or until a wooden pick inserted in the center comes out clean. Cool in pan for 10 minutes, then remove cups of cakes to a wire rack to finish cooling, which should take 30 minutes.

Chocolate Frosting:

1. Combine the butter, powdered sugar, and cocoa in the bowl of a stand mixer with the whisk attachment. For three minutes, beat at medium speed, scraping down sides as necessary, until the mixture is light and fluffy. Melted

chocolate, cream, and vanilla should all be thoroughly mixed in. Cover and chill for about 30 minutes or until just firm.

2. Stir the frosting before transferring it to a piping bag with a Wilton #21 fluted tip. Each cup of cake has a circle piped around its edge. Each chocolate frosting circle should contain coconut icing.

143. Rainbow Sheet Cake

Prep Time: 45 minutes

Cook Time: 30 minutes

Additional Time: 1 hour 15 minutes

Total Time: 2 hours 30 minutes

Servings: 10

Ingredients
Cake:

- ➤ baking spray with flour
- ➤ 1 cup of unsalted butter, softened
- ➤ 1 ½ cups of white sugar
- ➤ Three large eggs at room temperature
- ➤ 2 tsp. vanilla extract
- ➤ 3 cups of enriched bleached cake flour
- ➤ 1 tbsp. baking powder
- ➤ ½ tsp. kosher salt
- ➤ 1 cup of whole milk at room temperature

- ➤ gel food coloring: red or pink, orange, yellow, green, blue, and purple

Frosting:

- ➤ One (8 Oz.) package of cream cheese, softened
- ➤ ½ cup of unsalted butter softened
- ➤ 3 cups of powdered sugar, sifted
- ➤ 1 tsp. vanilla extract
- ➤ ⅛ tsp. kosher salt
- ➤ gel food coloring: red or pink, orange, and green

Directions

1. Amass all the ingredients.
2. Oven: 350 degrees Fahrenheit (175 degrees C). Spray parchment paper with baking spray before using it to line a 9x13-inch baking pan that has been greased.
3. Cake preparation For about 30 seconds, on medium speed, beat butter in a stand mixer with a paddle attachment until creamy. Gradually incorporate white sugar; beat for two to three minutes or until fluffy.
4. One at a time beat in the eggs just long enough to incorporate them after each addition—about a minute. Beat for about 15 seconds after adding vanilla to combine. Use a flexible spatula to clean the bowl's sides and bottom.
5. In a medium bowl, stir the flour, baking soda, and salt until well combined.
6. Beginning and ending with the flour mixture, add milk to the butter mixture alternately, beating each addition on low speed until combined.

7. In six small bowls, evenly distribute the batter. A drop or two of food coloring should be added to each bowl, and you should color one red or pink, one orange, one yellow, one green, one blue, and one purple. Gently combine, then, as necessary, add more coloring to achieve the desired shades.

8. The batter should be dropped into the prepared pan in alternating colors until the pan is full. [If you have extra batter, top off existing dollops of the same color rather than creating a second layer of different colors. Ensure the batter is evenly distributed and any gaps are filled by giving the pan a light tap on the counter.

9. Bake in the oven for about 30 minutes or until a toothpick inserted in the center comes out clean—15 minutes to cool in pan. The cake should be removed from the pan and allowed to cool completely on a wire rack for at least one hour.

10. Make the frosting: Blend the cream cheese and butter for about a minute on medium speed in a stand mixer with a paddle attachment. Slowly add the powdered sugar while keeping the mixer low, beating for about two minutes to incorporate. Increase the speed of the mixer to medium and beat for about a minute or until fluffy after adding the vanilla and salt.

11. Fill each of the three small bowls with 1/4 cup of frosting. One to two drops of food coloring should be added to each bowl, and one should be colored red or pink, one orange, and one green. Add additional coloring as needed and combine thoroughly to achieve the desired shades. Place the colored frostings in piping bags with tiny, round writing

tips. The remaining frosting should remain white in the mixing bowl.

12.   Trim the edges of the cake with a serrated knife.

13.   White frosting should only be used to frost the cake's top; leave the sides unfrosted.

14.   Create small rainbows on the cake's top using the colored frosting.

144. Best Mud Pie

Prep Time: 10 minutes

Additional Time: 8 hours 30 minutes

Total Time: 8 hours 40 minutes

Servings: 12

Ingredients

- 1 (6 Oz.) chocolate sandwich cookie crumb crust
- 1-quart coffee ice cream, divided
- 1 (12 Oz.) package of miniature chocolate chips
- 1 (12 Oz.) jar of hot fudge topping
- ½ (18 Oz.) package of crushed chocolate sandwich cookies divided
- 1 (8 Oz.) container of frozen whipped topping, thawed
- ¾ cups of chocolate syrup

Directions

1. About 30 minutes later, the crust should be firm.

2. In the meantime, pour half of the coffee ice cream into a bowl and give it 10 minutes to soften. Restore any leftover ice cream in the freezer. Ice cream that has softened and mini chocolate chips are combined. Over the frozen crust, spread the mixture evenly. Freeze for two hours while wrapped in plastic.

3. For about 30 seconds, warm up the fudge topping in the microwave on low until it is just warm enough to pour. Place in a bowl. For the garnish, set aside 2 tbsp. Of the biscuit crumbs, combine the remaining biscuit crumbs with the fudge topping.

4. After removing the pie from the freezer, place the fudge mixture over the ice cream layer. Wrap in plastic wrap and put back in the freezer for two hours.

5. The remaining coffee ice cream should be removed from the freezer and given 10 minutes to soften. Lay ice cream on top of the fudge layer. For another two hours, wrap it in plastic and return the dish to the freezer.

6. Spread whipped cream on the pie's top after removing it. To garnish, add the saved biscuit crumbs. Freeze for an additional two hours while wrapped in plastic.

7. Slice the pie into serving-sized pieces, then drizzle each with a tbsp. Or so of chocolate syrup.

145. Ube Cheesecake

Prep Time: 40 minutes

Bake Time: 1 hour 5 minutes

Cool Time: 2 hours 35 minutes

Refrigerate Time: 8 hours 20 minutes

Total Time: 12 hours 40 minutes

Servings: 10

Ingredients
Crust:

- cooking spray
- 1 cup of graham cracker crumbs
- 3 tbsp. unsalted butter, melted
- 1 tbsp. granulated sugar
- ⅛ tsp. kosher salt

Filling:

- 3 (8 Oz.), packages of cream cheese, softened
- ½ cup of granulated sugar
- 1 ¼ cups of ube jam (Ube Halaya)
- ½ cup of heavy whipping cream
- Three large eggs
- 2 tsp. ube extract
- ½ tsp. vanilla extract
- ¼ tsp. kosher salt

Ube Ganache

- ½ cup of white chocolate chips
- ¼ cups of heavy whipping cream
- ¼ tsp. ube extract

Directions

1. Oven: 325 degrees Fahrenheit (165 degrees C). Apply cooking spray sparingly to a 9-inch springform pan. Heavy-duty aluminum foil should be double-wrapped around the outside of the pan, extending up the pan's sides.

2. Crust preparation: Crumbs from Graham Crackers, melted Butter, Granulated Sugar, and Salt are combined in a bowl and thoroughly mixed in the bottom of the springform pan that has been prepared; press the mixture.

3. About 15 minutes into baking, check if the mixture is set and lightly golden. Put the dish on a wire rack for 20 minutes to cool.

4. Making the Filling: Cream cheese should be beaten on medium speed for about 2 minutes using a stand mixer with a paddle attachment. When there are no more streaks, add the cream and ube jam and beat until combined, occasionally pausing to scrape the sides and bottom of the bowl. One at a time, add eggs, beating each time only long enough to combine. Beat on low speed until combined before adding ube, vanilla, and salt. Filling is poured into the cooled crust.

5. Position the springform pan inside a sizable roasting pan. To halfway up the sides of the springform pan, pour hot water into the roasting pan.

6. Once again, bake in the preheated oven for 55 to 60 minutes, or until the center is almost set but still slightly wobbly. The oven should be turned off, and the cheesecake should be left in it for an hour with the door slightly ajar (about 3 inches).

7. Cheesecake should be taken out of the roasting pan and placed on a wire rack. After cooling the cheesecake for about an hour to reach room temperature, remove the foil from the pan's exterior. Put the container in the fridge for at least eight or twenty-four hours to chill completely. Cover with plastic wrap.

8. Ganache preparation In a medium heat-resistant bowl, put the chocolate chips in. When the cream in a small saucepan is steaming, pour it over the chocolate. Wait one minute, then whisk until the chocolate is smooth and melted. Ube extract should be added, then whisked in. Allow cooling for 15 minutes or until thickened.

9. Run a knife around the outside edge to unstick the cheesecake from the pan sides. Discard the pan's sides. Cheesecake should be moved to a serving platter or plate. Pour ganache over the cheesecake's top, letting it drip off the sides as it does so. Place in the fridge and chill for 20 minutes or until set.

146. TikTok Brownies

Prep Time: 10 minutes

Bake Time: 25 minutes

Cool Time: 45 minutes

Total Time: 1 hour 20 minutes

Servings: 16

Ingredients

- ½ cups of unsalted butter, plus additional for greasing pan
- ⅓ cups of cocoa powder
- 1 cup of granulated sugar
- 2 tsp. vanilla extract
- Two large eggs
- ½ cup of all-purpose flour

Directions

1. Three hundred fifty degrees Fahrenheit should be set for the oven (175 degrees C). Butter the inside of an 8x8-inch metal baking pan.
2. In a big pot over low heat, melt the butter. Take the pan off the heat and give it five minutes to cool. Add vanilla bean paste, sugar, and cocoa powder. Add eggs one at a time, stirring until combined. Add the flour and mix just enough to combine. Put the mixture in the pan that has been prepared and smooth the top.
3. Bake for 20 to 25 minutes in the preheated oven or until a toothpick inserted comes out clean.
4. After removing it from the oven, let it cool on a wire rack for at least 45 minutes before slicing.

147. Strawberry Crunch Cake

Prep Time: 40 minutes

Bake Time: 40 minutes

Cool Time: 1 hour 10 minutes

Chill Time: 1 hour

Total Time: 3 hours 30 minutes

Servings: 12

Ingredients
Cake

- baking spray with flour
- 2 ½ cups of all-purpose flour
- 3 tbsp. strawberry-flavored gelatin, such as Jell-O
- 1 tsp. baking powder
- 1 tsp. kosher salt
- ½ tsp. baking soda
- 1 cup of unsalted butter, softened
- 2 cups of granulated sugar
- Three large eggs
- 2 tsp. vanilla extract
- 1 ½ cups of whole buttermilk

Frosting

- 1 ½ cups of unsalted butter, softened
- ¼ tsp. kosher salt
- 1 tbsp. vanilla extract
- 4 cups of powdered sugar, sifted
- 2 tbsp. heavy cream, or more as needed

Crumble

- 25 golden Oreo cookies
- ⅔ cups of freeze-dried strawberries
- ⅛ tsp. Kosher salt4 tbsp. melted unsalted butter

Directions

1. Oven: 350 degrees Fahrenheit (175 degrees C). 2 (8-inch) round cake pans should have their bottoms lined with parchment and coated with baking spray and flour.
2. Combine the flour, gelatin, baking powder, salt, and baking soda in a bowl.
3. In a stand mixer bowl with the paddle attachment attached, beat butter for 2 to 3 minutes at medium speed until it is creamy. Gradually incorporate sugar while beating for three minutes or until light and fluffy. One at a time, add eggs, beating on low speed and stopping to scrape down the bowl's sides as necessary until just combined. Add vanilla and beat.
4. Buttermilk should be added in three additions, beginning and ending with the flour mixture, and beat on low speed until combined after each addition. Evenly distribute the batter among the prepared pans.
5. For about 40 minutes, bake in the oven until a wooden pick inserted in the center comes out clean.
6. Remove cakes from pans and let them cool completely on a wire rack for one to one and a half hours after cooling in the pans for ten minutes.
7. Butter and salt should be placed in the paddle attachment-equipped bowl of a stand mixer to make the frosting—3 minutes at medium speed to achieve a creamy consistency. Add vanilla and beat.
8. Powdered sugar and cream should be added gradually while beating slowly until fully incorporated and smooth. For 2 to

3 minutes, increase the mixer's speed to medium-high and beat it until it is smooth and fluffy.

9. Combine the cookies, strawberries, and salt in a food processor to make the Crumble. Pulse for 12 or until the mixture is slightly chunky and still has bits of biscuit and strawberry visible. Add the butter and pulse approximately five times to combine.

10. Using a serrated knife, smooth the tops of the cakes as necessary.

11. Place one cake layer on a serving platter and top with one cup of frosting. Add the final cake layer on top.

12. Apply the remaining frosting to the cake's top and sides.

13. Sprinkle Crumble over the cake's top and sides and gently press it into place until it is completely covered. Before cutting the cake, let it cool for an hour.

148. Ruffled Milk Pie

Active Time: 20 minutes

Bake Time: 45 minutes

Total Time: 1 hour 5 minutes

Servings: 8

Ingredients

➢ 12 tbsp. melted Ghee or clarified butter divided
➢ ¾ cups of granulated sugar

- ½ tsp. ground cinnamon
- ⅛ tsp. table salt
- 14 sheets of frozen phyllo dough, thawed
- One ¼ cup of whole milk
- ¼ cups of heavy cream
- Five large eggs
- 1 tsp. vanilla extract
- 1 tbsp. powdered sugar

Directions

1. Bake at 375 degrees Fahrenheit (190 degrees C). A 9 1/2-inch deep dish pie plate should have 1 tbsp. Butter is applied to the bottom and up the sides.
2. In a small bowl, mix the salt, sugar, and cinnamon.
3. Place one phyllo dough sheet on a clean work surface or cutting board and butter one side. Scrunch up the phyllo carefully by combining the short sides to form a rope.
4. Place loosely wrapped into a coil in the middle of the baking dish that has been prepared. Construct a concentric circle around the center coil using the remaining phyllo sheets and butter, packing them tightly as you go.
5. On top, scatter 2 tbsp. Of the spiced sugar mixture.
6. Bake for about 25 minutes or until golden in the preheated oven. Take the food out of the oven, then turn the heat to 325 degrees F. (165 degrees C).
7. While the phyllo bakes heat the milk and cream in a small saucepan over medium heat until it just begins to boil. Remove the heat.
8. In a bowl, combine the eggs, vanilla, and remaining spiced sugar mixture; constantly whisk as you add the hot milk

until thoroughly combined. Pour spiced milk over the phyllo in the baking dish immediately, then return the pan to the oven.

9. Bake the custard for 20 to 25 minutes until it is barely set. Sprinkle on some sugar powder—a warm or room-temperature serving is recommended.

149. Bananas Foster Cake

Prep Time: 30 minutes

Bake Time: 25 minutes

Cool Time: 1 hour 10 minutes

Total Time: 2 hours 20 minutes

Servings: 12

Ingredients
Banana Cake

> ➤ cooking spray
> ➤ 2 ½ cups of all-purpose flour
> ➤ 2 tsp. baking soda
> ➤ 1 tsp. table salt
> ➤ 2 cups of granulated sugar
> ➤ 2 cups of mashed banana (from 5 (6 oz.) bananas)
> ➤ 1 cup of canola oil
> ➤ ¾ cups of plain whole Greek yogurt
> ➤ ¼ cups of whole buttermilk

- ➤ 2 tsp. vanilla extract
- ➤ Two large eggs

Salted Banana Caramel Sauce

- ➤ 1 cup of dark brown sugar
- ➤ ½ cup of heavy cream
- ➤ ⅓ cups of unsalted butter
- ➤ ¾ tsp. ground cinnamon
- ➤ ¼ tsp. sea salt
- ➤ 1 ½ very ripe bananas, mashed
- ➤ ¾ tsp. vanilla bean paste or 1 1/2 vanilla beans
- ➤ 4 tbsp. dark rum, divided
- ➤ Three ripe bananas, sliced

Caramel Frosting

- ➤ 2 cups of unsalted butter, softened
- ➤ 4 cups of powdered sugar
- ➤ 1 cup of salted banana caramel sauce

Directions

1. The oven to 350 degrees Fahrenheit (175 degrees C). Cooking oil should coat three (8-inch) round cake pans, and parchment paper should line the bottoms.
2. In a sizable bowl, stir together the flour, salt, and baking soda. In a separate bowl, combine the sugar, yogurt, buttermilk, vanilla, eggs, 2 cups of mashed bananas, oil, and sugar; whisk to combine. Add the egg mixture to the flour mixture and stir just until combined. Assemble pans and distribute batter evenly among them.

3. When a toothpick is inserted and comes out clean, the baking should take 25 to 30 minutes in the preheated oven. Ten minutes are needed for pans to cool on a wire rack. Cakes should be removed from pans and allowed to cool on a wire rack for one to a half hours.

4. Sugar, cream, butter, cinnamon, and salt should all be combined in a small saucepan to make the caramel sauce. Cook for two minutes, constantly whisking over medium heat, until the butter has melted and the sugar has completely dissolved. Remove from heat, and add 3 tbsp. Of rum, 1 1/2 tbsp. Of vanilla bean paste and 1 1/2 bananas that have been mashed.

5. In a small bowl, combine the sliced bananas with the remaining 1 tbsp: of rum and 4 tbsp. of caramel sauce. Gently toss to combine. After about 20 minutes, bring the remaining caramel sauce to room temperature.

6. For the caramel frosting, beat butter in a bowl of a stand mixer with the paddle attachment on medium speed for about 3 minutes or until it turns light in color. Add the powdered sugar gradually, then beat the mixture at medium speed for about 3 minutes or until it is light and fluffy. Stir together for about a minute on low speed after adding 1 cup of the salted banana caramel sauce. Fill a piping bag with a #12 tip after transferring 1 cup of frosting.

7. To assemble the cake, place the first layer on a serving plate and top it with 2/3 cup of caramel frosting. The outer edge of the cake layer is decorated with a ring of caramel frosting piped using a piping bag.

8. Spread the frosting ring with the other half of the sliced banana mixture. Add the next layer of cake on top.

9. Add another 2/3 cup of caramel frosting to the second layer. Create a ring of caramel frosting with a piping bag by repeating the process around the outer edge of the cake layer.

10. Spread the frosting ring with the remaining banana-slice mixture. Finish with the final layer of cake.

11. Cover the cake's top and sides with the remaining frosting, spreading it evenly.

12. To decorate however you like, use a piping bag.

13. Slice and serve with any leftover 3/4 cups of caramel sauce.

150. Brownie Pie

Prep Time: 30 minutes

Freeze Time: 30 minutes

Chill Time: 1 hour

Bake Time: 45 minutes

Total Time: 2 hours 15 minutes

Servings: 6

Ingredients
Crust:

➢ One ¼ cup of all-purpose flour, plus more for rolling

- ➤ 1 tbsp. granulated sugar
- ➤ ½ tsp. kosher salt
- ➤ ½ cups of cold unsalted butter, cut into 1/2-inch pieces
- ➤ 3 tbsp. Ice water, or more as needed

Filling:

- ➤ 10 tbsp. unsalted butter melted and cooled
- ➤ ¾ cups of granulated sugar
- ➤ Two large eggs at room temperature
- ➤ One large egg yolk at room temperature
- ➤ 2 tbsp. canola oil
- ➤ 1 tsp. vanilla extract
- ➤ ¾ cups of unsweetened cocoa powder
- ➤ ½ cups of all-purpose flour
- ➤ 2 tsp. Instant espresso granules
- ➤ ½ tsp. kosher salt
- ➤ ½ cups of diced walnuts or hazelnuts
- ➤ ½ cups of semisweet chocolate chips, divided

Directions

1. In a food processor, add the flour, sugar, and tsp. of salt to make the crust. Pulse the ingredients three or four times to combine. Place cold butter on top of the flour mixture in the food processor. The butter should resemble pea-sized pieces after about six pulses. Over the butter mixture, drizzle 3 tbsp of water. If more ice water is required, add one tbsp. At a time until the dough forms beads resembling couscous.
2. Place the dough on a surface and press it into a single mass. Into a disc shape, flatten the dough.

3. For at least an hour or up to two days, wrap in plastic wrap and chill.
4. Take the dough from its packaging and set it on a work surface lightly dusted with flour. Ten minutes at room temperature will help the dough soften. Sprinkle flour over the dough's top. Roll the disc into a circle that is 12 inches in diameter using a rolling pin that has been lightly dusted with flour.
5. Place in a 9-inch pie plate, pressing down on the bottom and up the sides. Invert the edges and crimp them as desired. Freeze for 30 minutes while wrapped in plastic.
6. Oven: 350 degrees Fahrenheit (175 degrees C). Put parchment paper over the dough on the pie plate, then add dried beans or pie weights.
7. About 15 minutes into baking, the crust should start to set up.
8. Remove the parchment paper and pie weights before carefully removing the pie plate from the oven. Return the pie plate to the oven and bake for an additional 8 to 12 minutes, or until the crust is lightly golden brown.
9. Place on a wire rack and cool for 20 minutes until room temperature.
10. Melted butter, sugar, eggs, egg yolk, canola oil, and vanilla extract are combined in a bowl and whisked until well combined. Add salt, flour, instant espresso, and cocoa, whisking just until combined. Add 1/4 cup of chocolate chips and nuts.

11.   Scrap the mixture into the cooled crust, then smooth the top using a tiny offset spatula. On top of the pie, scatter the final 1/4 cup of chocolate chips.

12.   Bake in the preheated oven for 30 to 35 minutes, or until a toothpick inserted in the center comes out clean. If the crust turns too dark, cover it with aluminum foil. Twenty minutes should pass before serving.

Conclusion

In modern kitchens, the oven has grown in popularity. Both residential and commercial customers are buying this kind of oven more frequently.

Food can be prepared in various ways with the help of the oven. Typically, food cooks from the outside to the inside, and the oven spreads heat evenly throughout the food. Because of the oven's fans, the heat is distributed evenly throughout the food. By doing this, the heat evenly cooks the food on all sides and in all directions. In addition to enhancing the food's quality, this helps save time and energy. Convection ovens are often preferred over other types by many, which is one of the main reasons.

Many people also prefer ovens because the food prepared in them doesn't require water.

This is a major plus for those serious about maintaining control over their diets. Since water increases fat absorption into the blood, those who take diets seriously avoid adding water when cooking food.

An oven can cook food in various ways, including baking, roasting, and barbecuing. Notably, baking is the most typical way to prepare food in an oven. Many foods can be prepared in convection ovens. Ovens can cook various food, including meat, vegetables, fine bread, and delicate food. Convection ovens are used for baking and preparing fine bread because of their reputation for having delicate flavors and textures. Baking, roasting, toasting, and cooking are all possible uses for the oven. Food can be quickly prepared with the help of the oven.

Made in the USA
Monee, IL
30 April 2023

1989c523-593b-4646-ad74-57c7662b1669R01